First published by TabernacleINK PRESS 2025

Copyright © 2025 by Daniele Wilson

First edition

ISBN: 979-8-9988354-0-7

THINGS I WISH MY MOTHER TAUGHT ME

THE RITUALISTIC EMBRACE OF STEPPING INTO WOMANHOOD

BY

Daniele Wilson

This book is dedicated to: Unborn Daughter

I know you are coming. And you are exceptional, fierce, confident, and capable of more than people give you. You are not just beautiful, but you are also smart, loving, and kind. I had to learn a lot of these things on my own. But one of the reasons why I decided to write this book was because maybe, just maybe, you'll flourish in a way that was unimaginable for women in my generation. Unthinkable for the women in our family who came before you. You come from a long line of intentionally bright, intelligent, beautiful, and trailblazing women who didn't allow the world around them to dictate who they were and where they were going. I know you are coming into this world, kicking down doors and demanding your worth. Where my parents went, I will go farther; where they climbed, I will climb higher; and where I stop, you will continue. I wish you the best of luck on this journey called life. And I love you.

This book is dedicated to: Women like me

This book is also dedicated to all the women and young ladies in the world who have experienced immense spiritual warfare against their destinies. God wrote a book on every one of our lives and most of us have never asked him what is in that book. Because if we did, we would realize that we have been met with opposition against our destinies since the time of inception. The world expected and demanded that you fit into one circle. Choose a side and stick to it. This book is dedicated to that little girl inside who was always lost because society tells women how to dress, how to talk, and how to think. Many times, you didn't show up in the package that the world expected you to show up in. Because you always chose authenticity instead of conformity. This led to agitation, rejection, and controversy. You're welcome here. I'm sure that in this book, I've missed a million other things that could be discussed, but I hope this book validates your experience and gives you the courage to choose your true identity. May this book lift the veil and give you the fire to reach out to God to ask what is in your book. Because your warfare was not just warfare. It was an attempted abortion.

TABLE OF CONTENTS

Introduction

I would like to preface this book by saying this is not a self-help book. I'm not a guru. The Lord has taught me and led me on a self-discovery journey, which ultimately led to deep repentance and deliverance. I wanted to share what I've learned. I believe in taking the practical side of life and merging it with the spiritual side to achieve the most effective outcome. This book was written in two parts. I'm an engineer, and when we write code, we write the back end first and then write the front end. (Actually, you can write the front end simultaneously as you write the back end, but that's on a much larger scale.) I actually wrote the front end first and thought the book was completed. I wasn't aware it was not complete until the Lord took me deeper into him, which then allowed me to write the end. The end is what gave me absolute freedom. There is no real change without Jesus. Suppose you have been stagnating for years. Stuck in the same spot, but you desire to move. Time passes. Your environment changes. You get older, but you're still stuck; it's time to realize that spiritually, you are dwarfed. And the only one who can help your spirit grow is Christ.

Ephesians 6:12, *"For we wrestle not against flesh and blood, but against principalities, against powers, against the rulers of the darkness of this world, against spiritual wickedness in high places."* Our battles are very real, but in reality, they often manifest spiritually before they become physical, and unless we successfully uproot the spiritual root, our reality will never change. This book will not empower you to seek the physical benefits of thriving without spiritually fighting for your freedom in Christ. This book will not empower you to lean into your masculinity to conquer the world and gain respect. That's vanity. This is not a book for all the masculinas in the world who look at femininity as a weakness. That's foolish. This book is also not for women who are afraid of embracing themselves while facing their demons. I will not be advising you on how to dress or act so that people can accept you. This is a book of guidance and self-realization. I wish more of our moms had taught us these tools so we could better navigate such a cruel world.

This is a coming-of-age book—a testimony of sorts. One where womanhood is explored alternately, a way that isn't conventional for this current climate, but that is necessary for the average woman who is not interested in being put into one box. I'm not expecting that by the end of this book you will be an Amazonian woman, all confident and able to conquer the world. This is one tool. And honestly, this is years of lessons put into a few pages of a book. It took years to learn this information, so be patient with yourself.

A lot of the advice I will give in this book is based on things I learned independently through hard life lessons. The power of the spirit of God gave me insight into my personal trauma. Once I was mentally and emotionally ready, the spirit of God allowed me to heal, but gain wisdom and perspective about life and how best to navigate certain circumstances in life. I've always been extremely passive and soft spoken, and never really presented myself in this world in a way that allowed people to categorize me easily. Neither did I show up in the spiritual to fight for my freedom. I was a perpetual victim. This always caused issues for me because I was constantly being derailed and sabotaged in the spirit realm, and it manifested in the natural. This caused me to always find myself in some of the most uncomfortable positions in life, proving myself, my worth, and my credentials. The truth is, our destinies are always in question, and our paths are constantly being sabotaged by ruling spirits through people who can see through our stars what was written about us, who we are, and why we were born on this earth.

Out of my frustration, I began to pick up my sword (the word of God), and I started to inquire of the Lord for my freedom. That is when he taught me to fight for my freedom. *Psalm 144:1-2, "Blessed be the LORD my strength, Which teacheth my hands to war, and my fingers to fight: My goodness, and my fortress; My high tower, and my deliverer; My shield, and he in whom I trust; Who subdueth my people under me."*

This book explores the dynamics of human relations and human perception and analyzes the spiritual aspect of the cause, while taking life lessons and wisdom from those experiences, allowing you, the reader, the freedom to truly explore what and who you can be through Christ. But it is not selling you an idea that this transformation will be easy. This book is an ode to the power and authority God has, an ode to everything womanhood has to offer, and an exploration of the full spectrum of femininity. I began writing this book during a period of healing in my life. I'm still healing, learning, and growing, but this book makes all of my lessons worthwhile and tangible.

Listen, if I haven't convinced you to read this book yet, then consider this...Are you happy with how you see yourself today, or do you feel there is more to this thing called femininity? Do you constantly feel like you're being juggled around by people's expectations? Or that every time you feel like you caught your footing, someone gives you their opinion and you cave? If any of these apply to you, keep reading. If all of these apply to you, don't even think about putting this book down.

Chapter One: Learn to Talk to Yourself

"Have you realized that most of your unhappiness in life is due to the fact that you are listening to yourself instead of talking to yourself?" – Martyn Lloyd Jones

Psalm 103: 1-2 says *"Bless the Lord, O my soul: And all that is within me, bless his holy name. Bless the Lord, O my soul, And forget not all his benefits."* Here is an example of when David decided to speak to his soul. There are actually several psalms where he speaks to his soul. Often, we allow our thoughts to overpower us. To command the room. Shift our composure and breed doubt, fear, and confusion. Your soul, also known as your mind, where your thoughts and intelligence reside, tends to be hijacked by the evil forces in this world to subdue you into obedience to their will. Most times, your thoughts are not your own; it's like a computer virus that hijacked your computer through illicit sites or links. Because we were born into sin, the enemy can illegally hijack our thoughts to manipulate us. The reason why you need to speak to your soul (mind) is because, as a human vessel, you were created to be inhabited by a spirit—the spirit of God. But sin has created a dystopia where you can be inhabited by any spirit, multiple spirits, and they can even silence the spirit of God with their loud voices. Making your spiritual growth nearly impossible, making your physical life unstable. *James 1:8 A double-minded man is unstable in all his ways.* Part of asserting your dominion is silencing those voices by speaking to your soul. Taking captive thoughts that do not correlate with the word of God. *2 Corinthians 10:5 "Casting down imaginations, and every high thing that exalteth itself against the knowledge of God, and bringing into captivity every thought to the obedience of Christ."*

This will be a brief chapter. Learn to talk to yourself. Many of our internal thoughts can be clarified through self-conversations. This allows for self-evaluation and self-awareness. One thing I did learn from my mother was to talk to myself. I remember being a little girl, tiny, and walking in on my mom having full-blown conversations with herself. I used to think to myself, Wow. Such a strange lady. She's talking to herself. I subconsciously started doing it. I can't even tell you when I started. That's how long it's been. But I learned later in life that this became a superpower because I was able to shut out the noise of external feelings, emotions, and thoughts and zone into what I actually felt. Communicating out loud allows your thoughts to become clearer and gives you a chance to evaluate your actions and emotions to determine if they are valid or if you may have been overreacting. This trains you to correct yourself and challenge your own assumptions. Sometimes we are surrounded by so many people and their feelings and emotions that we take on their personalities, feelings, and ways of seeing the world, even when we ourselves do not share those perspectives or feelings. I remember in school I used to get made fun of because I didn't dress like all the other kids. The criticism and bullying were beyond palpable. I mean, let's quit school while we're at it, because I was over it. How many times can one young lady be a punching bag for other students? But every day, I would come home and talk through those experiences and evaluate how they made me feel. Sometimes you may not have the luxury to go to therapy or have parents or family members who listen and affirm your experiences. You may tend to be alone and captive in your mind. However, discussing experiences that you encounter provides a therapeutic outlet—one where you are not carrying all of this solitude or emotions on your shoulders.

That said, this is why aligning your thoughts with the word of God is so important. It's also important to remember that you are not actually alone. Spiritually, you are constantly being watched. God makes himself ready and available to listen. I remember not really understanding the power of prayer, but bringing my thoughts and emotions to God. Inviting him in allowed him the leeway to step in at times when my thoughts about myself were not accurate. I may feel this way about myself, but he thinks otherwise. I may have sensed something around me that I cannot quite explain, and in the middle of me holding a town hall meeting with myself, he comes in and validates my experience because I asked him what he thought. Our thoughts do not have to be as overpowering when we learn to talk to ourselves and when we allow God to do the heavy lifting.

Chapter Two: Speak Up for Yourself

OK, listen, we hear this a lot. Everyone says it. It's like a trend right now. *Speak up for yourself, advocate for yourself*...Blah blah blah...And the list goes on. But let's face it. How many of us as women have been taught to speak up for ourselves and advocate for what we want? I mean, men since the beginning of time have been raised to go for what they want and speak their minds. Be assertive—the whole gamete. However, women are often taught to be agreeable, understanding, selfless, and, above all, nice. Don't forget to be nice, because if you aren't nice, then you aren't feminine enough. Be nice! Even to your own detriment. And all we as women hear is...Be a doormat. Allow people to walk over you. Give too much of yourself because this is what being a woman looks like...If you are nice, people will like you, and men will find you feminine.

Let's begin by ruling out the misconceptions. Being nice does not mean you are not assertive. Being nice does not mean you do not speak up for yourself. Men weaponize our ability to be agreeable, understanding, selfless, and pleasant to get the best outcome for themselves. I am not saying you should never be any of these things. I am saying ensure that the environment where you are nice, agreeable, selfless, and understanding is a secure environment where you are allowed to grow. And that vulnerable part of you is protected and reciprocated. This goes beyond men; this flows into your interactions with people around you, non-romantically. That manager or boss who has no problem dumping all the workload onto your lap at the last minute, knowing that the deadline is coming up and you will be missing sleep and food to meet this deadline, is an example of a scenario where you should speak up and advocate for yourself. Or those fake girlfriends who do not check up on you. Or care about your personal feelings toward how they have treated you. Or who said something that overstepped boundaries with no apology toward you. Advocate for yourself. Discuss the incident and then express your concerns, because you matter too. Do not allow anyone to walk over you, dictating what kind of treatment you deserve. You can set boundaries and still be nice.

You won't be the type of woman that allows any and every one into your sacred space with their foolish-ness. And that's the truth. Individ-uals have a way of taking an inch and turning it into a mile because humans are inherently selfish.

Individuals have a way of taking an inch and turning it into a mile because humans are inheritably selfish.

Protect yourself. Get friends who are not offended by you simply saying, "Oh no, get somebody else to do it," or "This disturbs my peace." And get a significant other that is not insulted by you saying, "This does not serve me and I need change, or I won't continue to be here." Am I advocating for you to discard any and every one who is an inconvenience in your life? No. There is a difference between individuals making genuine mistakes who want to fix them and a person who has decided that you are not valuable enough for them to change how they handle and treat you. Over time, you will begin to notice the difference. Being agreeable, understanding, selfless, and nice requires an alkaline environment. Not one where you are forced into those traits out of survival, but one where it flows aimlessly from your inner self because the people around you are just as nurturing. Because those are high commodities and we mustn't be willing to freely give them out to any old Joe and Amanda.

My statements above were a general conversation for the masses. But here is what the Lord really showed me about myself. I want to share it because it's the secret to the "how." How do you speak up for yourself? The scenarios I mentioned above are symptoms of a larger issue that is actually occurring. The actual issue is rejection, paired with a tendency to people-please. You have been rejected, so you think people-pleasing will fix the rejection. Rejection is a spiritual attack that leads to frustration, silence, and stagnation. It leads to a million other things, too, but I won't touch on those here. However, the truth is that the enemy uses rejection to bind us. *Jeremiah 17:5 "Thus saith the Lord; Cursed be the man that trusteth in man, and maketh flesh his arm, and whose heart departeth from the Lord."* The real issue is that we are putting our trust in man more than God. Human opinions matter more to us than that still small voice that tells you no. Or the voice that tells you this is not a good idea; you should voice your concerns. We want to be accepted because we have experienced rejection so much from our family, the world, and ourselves. Now we even reject ourselves and refuse to advocate for our own well-being. Am I saying do not trust man? Not at all. But do not trust man above God. Yes, the Lord does send people into your life as checks and balances, but make sure those people's hearts have not departed from the Lord.

Because the actual issue is rejection and seeking approval from men through agreeability, you then put yourself in situations that cause you to be victimized. Rejection opens the door to trauma, abuse, and timidity, which are all ruling spirits by the way, and the strong man attached to those ruling spirits is the spirit of terror. The strong man is the ruling principality that the other spirits are subject to, or they are under that principality's command. Those spirits usually run in packs. You may have been traumatized for speaking up or bullied into silence and submission, which explains why it becomes difficult for you to speak up. As if there is a muzzle on your throat. Like you want to speak up, but you feel trapped. You have something to say, but now something is stopping you from defending yourself. Do you want to know how I know this? Because I was her. Speaking up became impossible, and if I did speak up, it came through me lashing out in anger and frustration because these entities were oppressing me through people. It became extremely difficult to find my voice.

I would first like to say that as long as you have Christ, you are safe. He is a strong man. All-powerful and very knowledgeable about your circumstances. Ask for his help and intervention. Request his guidance on how you can obtain freedom. What is holding my voice? My deliverance will look different than yours. I was able to find my voice after the Lord started teaching me that I must let go of my marriage to the world. I must let go of others' approval. I must let go of their criticism. I must cling to his word and what he says about me. I must value his voice more than I value the world's. All the way down to my parents. *Mathew 10:28 "And fear not them which kill the body, but are not able to kill the soul: but rather fear him which is able to destroy both soul and body in hell."* Because truth be told, they do not know everything. But God's spirit does. *1 Corinthians 2:10-12 "But God hath revealed them unto us by his Spirit:* **for the Spirit searcheth all things, yea, the deep things of God.** *For what man knoweth the things of a man, save the spirit of man which is in him? Even so the things of God knoweth no man, but the Spirit of God. Now we have received, not the spirit of the world, but the spirit which is of God; that we might know the things that are freely given to us of God."*

Understanding that the curses of trusting in man were rejection, double-mindedness, emotional instability, and losing my voice is what gave me the courage to begin to let go slowly. It's a slow journey that brings unfathomable freedom. Because there comes a time in your walk with God where your struggle is no longer speaking up to tell your boss that this workload is unfathomable for one person. Instead, it transcends to what if he sends you to speak to a nation that executes people on the spot for belief in Jesus Christ? What will you do? Will you choose silence because of fear of man? Or will your fear of God override your fear of man and propel you to usefulness? Because our voices are weapons. And even writing this book, I

29

had to choose total obedience. I could not fear that people would crucify me for writing what the Lord laid on my heart. Choose freedom! Choose peace!

Chapter Three: Embrace Your Villain Era

We have just finished discussing the importance of being nice, agreeable, and amicable, as well as the environment in which these traits are necessary for thriving. Entering our villain era, on the other hand, is a rite of passage. When I mention villain era, it does not mean you become a villain. I want to clarify that for the people in the back. It means your environment will begin to perceive you as a villain because you have broken out of a mold that others wish to break out of. You have found your voice when the world around you is still caged. Standing up for oneself and being so-called bossy or mean is not the same as being hard to deal with. But the world will make you believe it's the same thing, and therefore, the connotation will be negative. In this chapter, I am going to break down why your assertiveness will be perceived as bad in comparison to being forced into amicability for the sake of peace. We will also discuss how you are negatively motivated to step out of boundaries and personal advocacy in exchange for a more positive view of how the people around you perceive you.

You may be assertive, have boundaries, have standards for yourself, or even dress a certain way, and people will perceive you as rude and defiant. Your boundaries, assertiveness, and standards are perceived as so much of a threat that they are often equated with being the bad guy. This is brainwashing one-on-one and forcing you, as a woman, to associate advocating for yourself as negative. Don't allow a THEM problem to become a YOU problem. Playing nice to get along when the overall objective is compliance is...suffocating.

The reality is that anytime a woman may in advertently offend someone, she is then perceived as a villain. The offense may or may not be a real offense. A woman who is usually straightforward, headstrong, and direct causes offense. A woman

A woman that chooses to speak truth will be offensive and a woman that doesn't cower, will also be offensive.

who chooses to speak truth will be offensive, and a woman who doesn't cower will

also be offensive. This offense is then used to categorize that woman as everything negative, labeling her unpleasant. Being labelled as the bad guy, when necessary, comes with the territory. There are scenarios in life where you have to stand firm and step on some toes.

This goes beyond being assertive. Sometimes people will play in your face, invalidate your experience, or even try to silence you. This is when the lioness comes out. It's a defense mechanism that you must learn, because if you don't, you will always get swallowed up and spit out by people who have bigger balls and more audacity than you. Dare I say, as I am writing this, that being a villain, when necessary, has everything to do with how audacious you are. And trust me, this is a trait that you develop. Because if you wait for people to give you what you deserve or permit you to inhabit your complete form, you will be sadly disappointed. No one will ever give you that kind of permission.

Sometimes you do have to come into a room, kicking down doors and demanding respect. It's not rude when the people in the room always wait until you specifically have something to say to get their point across. I mean, every time I have a new idea, you all of a sudden have something to say? Where was all of this brilliance during the brainstorming period of our meeting, when there was no benefit to you to embarrass me or show off how much more intelligent you are (or what you recognize to be intelligence)?

Please...have several seats. We have all encountered many of these moments, and you will encounter many more in your life. From play dates to group projects in school to corporate America. You know what? Let's take it a step further, to that hairstylist who said she could do that hairstyle you found on Instagram. Yes, her. Tell her you are not paying for the gibberish she put on your head unless she undoes it and redoes it exactly like the picture, or gives you a full discount or refund because we are tired of taking things to the chin to appease people who sleep peacefully at night, even though they have done some of the most egregious things to their fellow humans. That sauce is what adds flavor to the stew called you. Embrace it, because honestly, it will save you from moments in life where you really are the victim.

I would like to add that the real problem with your interactions with people may not be anything natural, but rather a spiritual issue. If you look through patterns in your family, how many of your family members are always experiencing pushback, no matter where they work, how nice they are, and how accommodating they are? I wrote the latter part of this before learning that there is such a thing as the spirit of reproach, which can affect yourself, your family, or both. The spirit of reproach is an enemy of progress. It causes you or your family to be objects of criticism, shame, and scorn, a scapegoat, and constantly discredited. There is no honor with reproach. No matter how nice you are or how gifted you tend to be. Those spirits manipulate your life and cause you to always find yourself on the outer courts of people's approval. It affects work, school, relationships, and even your personal and professional life. Do you trust in man's approval? No. But as children of God, we should be favored among men. *Proverbs 3:4 "So shalt thou find favour and good understanding in the sight of God and man."*

As you begin to pray more and yield to God's influence and his dominion (Because that is very integral to your freedom and deliverance), there is no deliverance without prayer, and if anyone tells you otherwise, they are liars.) You will notice that your influence with men will also change. People who oppose God will oppose you, and people who love the Lord will love you. Praying against the spirit of reproach, stagnation, and regression over yourself and your family spiritually makes a big difference that also yields effects in the natural. *Isaiah 54:4 "Fear not, for you will not be ashamed; be not confounded, for you will not be disgraced; for you will forget the shame of your youth, and the reproach of your widowhood you will remember no more."*

Chapter Four: Embrace Your Femininity and Sexuality

Femininity can have very nuanced meanings. This can be very difficult to pinpoint, especially in a society where femininity is villainized and sexuality is exploited. A woman's femininity is the very thing that makes this world go round. It's this sacred formula that God gave us for not only surviving but thriving. It's not a weakness or a negative point; it's our superpower. Femininity

Femininity is soft, in tune with that still voice called intuition, it's quiet. allows you as a woman to shapeshift into spaces smoother than most and can be used so much to your advantage that wars have been started in the past because of it. Femininity is soft, in tune with that still voice called intuition. It's quiet. And when I say quiet, I don't mean literal quiet. I mean quiet

39

as in femininity doesn't have anything to prove. Femininity is carefree and playful. Have I gotten more out of life by presenting in a feminine way to the world? Yes. Has that made me a target at times by womanizing men, gnawing and gnashing of the teeth type women, and the black hole that we call corporate America? Also yes. But it's not because of what you think.

The truth is, femininity is attacked when it comes to women, just as masculinity is attacked when it comes to men. It's a spiritual concept; the enemy attempts to overthrow the system of God and establish his own system where everything is backwards. Everything is upside down. What is good is bad, and what is bad becomes good. The Lord established femininity in women for the purpose of creating an ecosystem where life is created and then nurtured to fulfillment. The male may hold the seed that contains the potential for what could be. But the woman has the soil that contains all the nutrients that are needed to grow and nurture the potential of a seed into its complete form. Somehow, this society has created an imbalanced ecosystem where femininity has been poisoned. No longer is it deemed necessary to cultivate that softness that God created. Because this world has developed its own ecosystem where things that carry no life and nurture nothing are elevated to the top and advertised as the epitome of womanhood. As a matter of fact, femininity is all but thrown out the window.

Remember, I stated that femininity is a superpower? Femininity can allow you to be a quiet storm. One where femininity shields your strength and attributes, allowing you to observe as much as possible in your environment and take as much information in as needed. So that when you are ready to execute, no one sees it coming. Many women are taught to fight for their place in society. Make men your job, and women respect you. Prove your worth! Show them who you are! But for what? That's wasted energy. *1 Peter 5:6 "Humble yourselves therefore under the mighty hand of God, that he may exalt you in due time."* Because I have begun to understand that this world is merely a victim of the spiritual realm, I have started to wait on the Lord. Waiting on the Lord is bringing your petitions to him, understanding that he is the one who shifts mountains, and your faith is the currency with which your request stands. *Philippians 4:6 "Be anxious for nothing, but in everything by prayer and supplication, with*

41

thanksgiving, let your requests be made known to God."

Anxiety ages you, darling. The Lord created women in such a way that we thrive in ease. Meaning there is only so much stress and anxiety and worry that we can carry before our bodies begin to rebel. You can achieve the same goals sitting comfortably and resting in your femininity. And look better doing it too. All this physical fighting ages you. Fight in prayer. Find your voice through prayer. Allow the Lord to pour into you and nurture you so you can nurture your ecosystem. Flow in life.

If femininity is like air—providing oxygen for the ecosystem, felt, but never seen—then sexuality is like a stream of water. It collects oxygen and attracts living things for hydration. But too much of it causes death. The truth is, a lot of us have not been taught properly about our sexuality, and it has been ill-managed through programming...and femininity and sexuality are not the same thing. Sexuality is a pheromone you exude. She whispers. She's not a villain. She's something God himself gave you to attract your mate. She's not meant to be explored with multiple partners because they sully her essence. She belongs to you (your husband and you.)

Sexuality cannot flow from sex appeal because sexuality has nothing to do with sex appeal. In this generation and before us, sexuality has been paired with vulgarity and reprogrammed to flow from sex appeal. When in reality sexuality is meant to be hidden and sacred. It operates within the confines of safety and is not intended to be exploited by the world. Remember, sexuality whispers to entice one mate. She whispers...The reason why sexuality does not flow from sex appeal is that sex appeal is rooted in vanity. It's fleeting and attached to lust. Sex appeal is a person exploiting the lust of the eyes and lust of the flesh to create a reaction from another person to entice them. Sex appeal is manipulation. Sexuality is neither the former nor the latter. It doesn't rise from sex appeal but from that raw essence that God placed inside of you as a woman.

Your sexuality rests in your femininity. There is a particular pheromone that you exude when you are sleeping in your femininity and have embraced your sexuality. Does this mean post it all over the internet for the world to see? No. We are discussing using your sexuality to empower you, not using it as a crutch for your self-esteem issues. There is a difference. I grew up thinking that sexuality was a negative. Only *loose ladies of the night* embraced their sexuality, and you had to be dressed super provocatively to accept your sexuality. In reality, accepting and understanding your sexuality is an internal thing, and as stated above, has nothing to do with your sex appeal. It has everything to do with how confident you are in your body, how you view yourself, and how you accept how you were created.

Can this world and its desires taint sexuality? Yes. This world's desires can taint sexuality. From the fountain of this world, you can drink this world's waters and taint your sexuality. The easiest way to protect your sexuality or recover it is through purging from the influences of this world through Christ.

Femininity and sexuality pair to create a beautiful harmony if both are respected and both are protected. The goal with femininity and sexuality is to have them work together to give off a quiet but strong and reassuring fragrance when you walk into the room. Choose clothes that reflect this confidence. Make eye contact, smile, tilt your head ever so slightly, and be confident. You have the formula; what else do you have to prove?

Chapter Five: Learn to Distinguish When You Are the Problem and When the Problem Is Around You

We are getting to the accountability part of my sermon. Part of your evolution will be distinguishing between two things. The unadulterated truth is that it is not always the outside world. Sometimes you are the problem. Bitterness, anger, unforgiveness, and rejection are just a few spirits that spawn from unhealed trauma and came in early. Some even since your conception. Some have been passed down through generations. They have been manipulating your growth and stagnating your life. Causing friction after friction with yourself and the people around you making you

Self-accountability and self-evaluation are necessary for your metamorphoses.

unable to heal or evolve past your trauma. And if you look at your family, you will notice the same pattern. *Hebrews 12:15 "looking carefully lest anyone fall short of the grace of God; lest any root bitterness springing up cause trouble, and by this many become defiled."* Unhealed wounds skew your lenses and stop you from seeing the world how it really is. At times, you are attracting the drama, or you are allowing people to abuse you. Healing is essential to your growth. Self-accountability and self-evaluation are essential for your metamorphoses.

Here is the formula for healing: forgiveness and letting go of offense. Offense is feelings of hurt, resentment, or anger that occur when someone feels wronged, insulted, or mistreated. It comes from perceived or actual actions, words, or behaviors that violate one's personal expectations, values, or boundaries. This leads to a range of emotional reactions such as resentment, anger, hurt, and unforgiveness. And unforgiveness is simply an unwillingness to let go of the offense.

Hear me out: You have two layers of forgiveness. You have the first layer where current situations took place, and you are willing to let it go and forgive. But there are some wounds that you feel like are so egregious because of what a person did, and forgiveness is letting the person off the hook. So, you ponder the offenses, analyze and meditate on the pain and the instance, and you garner resentment. Whether it's toward your parents, family, or friends. You feel as if they have to pay, and they are not deserving of forgiveness. But here is the truth. Unforgiveness is expensive. Not for the culprit. But for you. The emotional weight and baggage your body holds because of the pain you refuse to release keep you in bondage spiritually, emotionally, and physically. And for some of you, you've already heard this, but it's too painful to forgive. This is when Christ comes in. You can't forgive to the extent you need to without him. Because some of this pain is buried, you wouldn't even be able to access it without him revealing it to you. But this is why he's here. A counselor. John 14:26-27, *"But the Advocate, the Holy Spirit, whom the Father will send in my name, will teach you all things and will remind you of everything I have said to you. Peace, I leave with you; my peace I give you. I do not give to you as the world gives. Do not let your hearts be troubled and do not be afraid."* The first step of forgiveness is admitting that you have a grudge. A grudge may be so well hidden that you forgot it. That's why you have to ask Christ to help you find any unforgiveness in your heart and help you examine the pain and damage. This may take days, weeks, months, and even years, especially when the trauma is deep.

Write down the people, the places, and the things. Go down memory lane with God. It might be too painful, but in order to progress forward, you must uncover your past. DIG!! Ask the hard questions. Cry. Wrestle with what took place, but your heart posture must be set on making a decision to forgive. You may not know how today. You may not even want to. But first, make the decision that you will forgive. And then begin to go down memory lane. Uncovering the hidden pain. When you are ready, give it to him in prayer. You may not even have words in that instant. It may simply be a deep cry from within, but release everything. And when you recall some more, release it. Forgiveness is a personal choice. It's a decision that is not grounded in your emotions or how you feel. It's rooted in desiring a deep level of freedom that can only be found in forgiveness.

When dealing with offense, since it is continual, get into the habit of telling God how you feel before you share it with others. He's always listening. Tell him how whatever took place hurt your feelings and made you feel upset or sad, and then allow him to comfort you. It may be a still small voice, or a sense of peace, or simply a weight being lifted off your shoulders. But don't let that offense linger within you to poison you and make you bitter. Hebrews 12:15, *"See to it that no one falls short of the grace of God and that no bitter root grows up to cause trouble and defile many."* And believe you me, bitterness is more common than you think. Everyone has it. There may be a small percentage of people who don't, because they are constantly in God's presence, giving Him their pain. And a smile and being happy or having "joy" doesn't mean you aren't bitter. I've learned that no matter how cheerful I was, how positive I was, or how kindly I treated people, I was still a very bitter person. Because bitterness does not always look like it is portrayed in movies, it's not necessarily the person wearing all black or the wicked stepmother in Snow White. Bitterness is rooted when you leave pain untreated and eventually taints the way you deal with yourself, the people around you, and God. If you have any unresolved pain, you are seen as bitter in God's eyes.

And the last step to managing forgiveness and offense is humility. I have learned an added dimension of humility that I was not taught in church. The spirit of God had to teach me this and shift my perspective. Humility is not of this world. It's not natural to us as humans. Our natural disposition is pride. We live, breathe, and eat pride, hence why pride is so prevalent in the Bible, but also prevalent in this world—the pride of life. And for the record, false humility is pride. *1 John 2:16 "For all that is in the world, the lust of the flesh, and the lust of the eyes, and the pride of life, is not of the Father, but is of the world."* Pride is not only rooted in self-reliance but also in idolatry.

Idolatry of self. Self-worship to be exact. Humility is the detachment from self-worship and attachment to the worship of God. That is what *1 Peter 5:6 "Humble yourselves therefore under the mighty hand of God, that he may exalt you in due time"* means. If we begin to worship God, worship is the exaltation of one. If we start to worship God instead of exalting ourselves, our focus shifts to the greater one. The higher one. The creator. The life giver. The source. And that worship, as we begin to realize exactly who he is, is where we will find our identity. In him, we find ourselves. That is humility. As we start to know him, we realize how prideful we are. How is it possible that the creator who was never created—The source. The father of spirits. The epitome of infinite power and authority—that he is whole. He needs nothing. He is self-sustaining. How is it possible that he came down here as a baby? A carpenter, taking orders from his father as a boy. The creator. Living his life to be slaughtered as a lamb. Knowing where he was going, he still chose to love and forgive. He still decided to lay his life down. He could've sent legions of angels. But he yielded. Have we ever thought about how it is to have absolute power, a puff of your breath, and you can kill every human that exalts themselves above you? But you exhibit grace and mercy. Have we ever considered what that looks like? Because truth be told, if we were him, every time a human uttered foolishness, we would send down lightning. We would've come to earth as a tall, handsome king with riches and an entourage to flex our power and authority. Self-worship.

What kind of God is this? As you meditate on him. As you draw to him. As you communicate with him in prayer. You will begin to cry because he helps you become more like him. Because humility is not of this world. Yield the desire to want to get even and SHOW THEM. It's vanity. Learn to forgive quickly; it keeps your heart pure and your energy sacred. Let go of offense. Cast down your crown. *Revelations 4:10-11 "the twenty-four elders fall down before him who sits on the throne and worship him who lives for ever and ever. They lay their crowns before the throne and say: "You are worthy, our Lord and God, to receive glory and honor and power, for you created all things, and by your will they were created and have their being.""*

Some of the most gracious women have some of the worst horror stories. But what

54

brought them through the fire was their ability to remain realistic, let go of offense, and forgive. If you are on fire, own it! There is no sense in blaming the next person for being on fire, unless that person set you on fire. But even then, it's too expensive to remain lit on fire, blaming the person. Instead, you should be figuring out a way to free yourself. Sometimes our fires are fueled by ignorance, self-loathing, insecurity, low self-esteem, and a lack of maturity. And that's OK, because that is why you have picked up this book to read. To gain a little wisdom.

Realism allows you to pinpoint the problem so you can allow God to fix it. Address yourself head-on. He is vulnerable with God. Call yourself out! And guess what, giving God permission to call you out and hold you accountable covers your blind spots. He does speak, if you would be patient enough to listen. You could never imagine how many times in my quiet time with him, he revealed some of the wildest things about me. I couldn't even believe it. But because he's the spirit of truth, he said what he said, so I take his word for it. Because if you focus on fixing your backyard, you won't have time to be roped into anyone else's mess. This self-work allows for a level of maturity and growth that only comes through accountability. Have you ever seen older women who are stuck in the same rut because they make the same mistakes over and over, all because they refuse to say, Enough is enough? Time is valuable. Maximize it. Own it and embrace it. Learn from your mistakes and accept the consequences of your choices and decisions. No one can ever expose you if you have already exposed yourself to yourself.

There are times when people's behaviors are entirely out of your control, and how they treat you has everything to do with their inner demons. You are not responsible for that. Self-accountability allows you to notice when you are wrong and when someone else is wrong. Don't ever let the outside world confuse you with either. Nine times out of ten, the world will say it's you when sometimes it simply is not you. The microaggression is not your fault. Someone devaluing you is not your fault, and you never being good enough for a certain friend group or man, is NOT YOUR

FAULT! Say it with me. It's not my fault. That is an internal issue that they must resolve outside of you. And in the meantime, you will remove yourself (unless the spirit of God says otherwise) because the healed, more sophisticated, and gracious you cannot remain around this kind of energy. Once you begin to evolve, you will realize you have outgrown a lot of your old friend groups and men that you would've previously dated. And even your workplace.

Get a good therapist. One that helps you balance reality and your insecurities. Therapy is simply your soul and spirit looking for another human to validate and analyze your human experience. Therapy allows you to heal in a most wholesome way. Therapy is like entering a cluttered room with boxes, clothes,

Therapy allows you to hold space for this pain but then gives you the opportunity to hold the door open in front of

and paper everywhere and you hire an organizer to help you declutter and clean up this room. A good therapist helps you figure out what is

57

you to walk away from it and move seamlessly through life. important, what is not worth your mental bandwidth, and what is worth letting go.

Freedom, mental freedom, is more important than the weight of the pain and trauma that the people around you have caused. Therapy allows you to hold space for this pain, but then allows you to hold the door open in front of you to walk away from it and move seamlessly through life.

The most important part of this chapter is to allow God to reveal you to you and will enable him to heal you. This chapter is heavy lifting and requires a power stronger than you. One that is omnipresent and all-knowing and has infinite knowledge. *2 Chronicles 16:8 "For the eyes of the Lord run to and from throughout the whole earth, to shew himself strong in the behalf of them whose heart is perfect toward him."* He searches all things. Including you. *Jeremiah 17:9-10 "The heart is deceitful above all things, and desperately wicked: who can know it? I the LORD search the heart, I try the reins, even to give every man according to his ways, and according to the fruit of his doings."* Allow him to search you for true healing.

And I'll tell you a secret. He knows. He is aware. And he cares. I grew up hearing that without experiencing it. But for the first time in my life, I'm beginning to experience it. I remember one morning I woke up with a heavy heart. I was fatigued by people and their lack of empathy for me. I had just received life-changing news and did not know how to process it except through grief. I was talking to God about how I felt abandoned and lonely by the people around me, including my husband. At the same time, my father in heaven was communicating to my husband to come into the room and was downloading how I truly felt. My husband went into the room and tended to me as if I had given him a manual on my grief. The Lord put my grief in better words than I could've and helped him understand. In that moment, I understood how when the Lord says he is near. He is near. When he says I am a friend. He is a friend. When he says he will protect and defend. I understood in that experience that no. He is no man that should lie. Trust him and allow him in to help.

Chapter Six: Your Self Security, Confidence, and Self Love Will Be a Threat to the People Around You

This is the one! I mean, if this isn't the one, I don't know what to tell you! When you choose to do the internal work to become the woman you envision, you decide to partner with God for excavation. You first begin by uprooting a lot of things that were commonplace for you and starting over. This is what true deliverance means. And this is the freedom that our architect in heaven designed when he sent Jesus down here to liberate us from bondage. Your metamorphosis is similar to doing a complete rehab on a home. First, you have to assess the damage, knock the home down to the studs, estimate how much the full rehab will cost, and then start rebuilding. Once you rehab that old shanty of a house, the new home looks so good you wouldn't believe it was the rusty old house you bought at a discount price that nobody wanted. Now all of a sudden, everyone is asking you where you got your marble tile and how much this and that cost. That is the same thing that happens internally within you. The process will be painful, long, and brutal, but once you allow the Lord to rebuild (a key word: allow Him to rebuild, because He is a restorer and redeemer, and you don't have the tools to rebuild), your beauty will radiate both internally and externally. Your worth automatically goes up. And do you know what that does to people around you? People who have known you all your life as x, y, z? You were always this or that in their eyes. Now you have glowed up. The price has shot up and your confidence and security are second to

That can be scary to people in your life who measured their worth and value based off of your shortcomings and your inadequacies.

none. Especially if you partner up with God for this demolition project and allow him to rebuild, your confidence, security, and identity now rest in him and who he said you are and would be. You no longer have to define your self-worth or fight for scraps of validation from a fallen world. Because the one that holds the world by the power of his

63

word, *Hebrews 1:3 The Son is the radiance of God's glory and the exact representation of his being, **sustaining all things by his powerful word**. After he had provide purification for sins, he sat down at the right hand of the Majesty in heaven. The one that knew you before you were born. Jeremiah 1:5 "**Before I formed you in the womb I knew you**, **before you were born I set you apart**; I appointed you as a prophet to the nations."* The one that is all truth *John 16:13 But when he, the Spirit of **truth**, comes, he will guide you into all the **truth**. He will not speak on his own; he will speak only what he hears, and he will tell you what is yet to come.*

He defined you. He validated you. He redeemed you. Meaning his word holds weight. If he were to lie, all things (the world) would collapse. That means you are free from the rat race of proving yourself because your stamp of approval comes from heaven.

That can be scary to people in your life who measure their worth and value based on your shortcomings and your inadequacies. They always thought they were better than you because they had the latest clothes or shoes, and you wore clearance items. They were always invited to all the exclusive events, and you weren't. They were up here, and you were always down there. It was funny to them that you could never catch up. Oh, poor baby, they would say and laugh in private with their friends. Their charity case. Maybe you noticed it, or perhaps you didn't. I know I never really noticed it until I noticed it (healing will do that to you). Imagine now they have to see you constantly crushing your environment and catapulting to a level they never saw for you, in a way that is more than superficial.

This is very similar to people whom you haven't known you all your life, but you may have just met or work with, and they underestimate you. Now they are fuming because how dare you have the audacity. But that's a them problem, not a **YOU** problem. Do not allow the people around you to make you feel like you are too much, and you should dim your light. Do not allow fear to intimidate you from those people. Because there is never enough dimming you can do to make an insecure person feel secure. I've been told several times I should humble myself. How do I humble myself when I haven't even said a word

Because there is never enough dimming you can do to make an insecure person feel secure

since I've entered the room. It's not what you say, it's that confidence that is radiating through your pores and bothering them. They will not support this transition. They will not show you an outpouring

of love. Some of them will even try to sabotage. And others may try to ride your coattails because it benefits them, not because they are truly ecstatic for you. They will watch your social media pages and not like a single picture. They might even invite you to outings just to throw jabs at your newfound confidence. Beware that it is in this moment that you realize who your real friends are, and some of us will know we didn't have any friends to begin with. But don't fear, this new version of you will attract some of the most beautiful people you will ever meet.

They can try as hard as they may to pop your bubble. Don't let them, because you would be allowing the enemy to overthrow the work that the Lord is doing in you. The Lord and you have worked too hard to be this secure in who you are. Hold on to him. Abide in him. *John 15:4 "Remain in me, as I also remain in you. No branch can bear fruit by itself; it must remain in the vine. Neither can you bear fruit unless you remain in me."* Because you cannot bear fruit outside of him, the currents are too strong. The environment is too harsh. Even if you crumpled up into a doormat and lay on the floor for them to walk over you, that still wouldn't be enough for them. It wouldn't solve whatever issue they have with you. The problem isn't with you; it's within them. They are upset that you have mustered up the courage to ask for more in your life. Go with peace, darlin', and live your life. The sky is the limit, and you don't have time to entertain negativity. The only thing you should be doing is stopping to smell the roses and taking the sunshine in. Good riddance to anyone who opposes.

Chapter Seven: Men Are Not to Be Chased Because They Are Not the prize

Listen... And listen very carefully. If your mother never taught you this, let me be the first woman to tell you. Men are not the prize! No matter how many YouTube videos they make, podcasts they host, books they write about their excellence and value, they are not the prize. Say it with me. Men are not the prize. I felt the need to reiterate that a million times because, as women, we are taught that we are nonexistent and insubstantial until we have a man in our lives. Are there benefits to having a man in your life? Yes, just like there are benefits to having a Chanel.

As women, we have to stop making men idols. You can idolize a man, and then when you marry him, you dishonor and disrespect him. Making a man an idol does not mean you will honor or respect him and his leadership. It simply means you have prioritized worship of a man and

69

the status of marriage above the almighty God. And I've heard several preachers use this scripture to discuss Jezebel and women's lack of submission. But I wanted to explore an interesting lens that my attention kept being drawn to. Genesis 3:16 says, *"To the woman he said, 'I will make your pains in childbearing very severe; with painful labor you will give birth to children.* ***Your desire will be for your husband***, *and he will rule over you.'"*

OK, stay with me, because I am about to go down a rabbit hole that explains a lot of our conflicts and bondage we have as women. When this scripture is discussed, the statement "***Your desire will be for your husband***" is spoken as a curse. The Lord spoke several curses because of Eve's disobedience, and I thought it was so interesting that the verse said your desire shall be for your husband. I was confused for a second because that didn't make sense. Why would that be spoken as a curse? Aren't you supposed to desire your husband? I started researching, but all the sermons I fell across were regurgitations of the same old tired message that women desire to rule over their husbands, but their husbands will rule over them. I will rely on the spirit of God to help crack this open for me once again.

Your desire in Hebrew is (tə·šū·qā·t̪ê̱ḵ), meaning **a longing**. **Will be for** is (wə·'el-) meaning **near, with, among, to**. Our issue is our idolatry of men. We idolize the concept of having a man, being with a man, marrying a man, and most of us sacrifice our youth for men, some women their children to men, through allowing any man into their homes and access to their children, and we sacrifice our dignity for men. And God did not intend it to be that way. We are so precious to him. Flowers that are delicate and should only be given to the deserving. That's how he created us. He intended marriage as a beautiful covenant to display his kingdom on earth. But because we live in a fallen world, most women do not even marry the men with whom they engage themselves, or give children to, or give birth to children for. And if we are honest and reflect on our actions, our idolatry causes us to sacrifice on the altar of men. And once our idols disappoint us, we find ourselves needing to repair the damage, doing a shoddy job. Once our idols disappoint us, we find ourselves in bitterness and pain, and now need to assume independence that leads to insurrection and lawlessness and ultimately rebellion to the structure God created. God never intended for us to be this way. If God is primary in our lives, we will follow his commands first, which means we are searching for a man who resembles Christ on earth (a lion and a lamb). Secondly, we would wait and seal our covenant with God, and then have intercourse after the covenant has been established, not before. And then we would respect and honor our leadership through submission because we trusted God to give us a worthy son who resembles him. Instead, our idolatry leads us to being rulers in our own lives and choosing men based on our lust, greed, and rebellion, and we suffer the consequences of what happens when we rule our own lives.

Here's the truth: men are not gods. They are humans; they make mistakes, fall short, get tired, and disappoint. If we take them off this pedestal of what we think they are supposed to be, we open up the door to pour out more grace on our fathers and our husbands. Take your father off the pedestal you placed him on and remove your husband or any other man you have idolized from their pedestal, and engage with who they are. There is no perfect man. This is for my girlies who are dating. There is none. You know what the Lord told me while I was dating my husband, and he had shortfalls, and I lacked mercy? God told me, "Every man has flaws, you will leave and will find another man with something else."

Does this mean tolerate being in a relationship with someone with whom you have different values and beliefs, or who mistreats you? No, that's not what I am saying. Different values and beliefs and abuse are not the same as seeing the humanity of a being. This is for the daughters who are hurting and broken because their first heartbreak came from their father. And the wives who have built resentment toward their husbands because he was not what they imagined he should be. And for the girlies who find any little flaw that is not foundational, and make it foundational. Give them mercy. Give them compassion. And forgive them and release them from the prison you put them in. And interact with them through the lens of Christ. See them as Jesus sees them. Because that is how God interacts with us, and we reflect him.

The reality of the situation is that when Adam was created, God felt like something was missing. And that something was you, darling. Things don't shake or move until you enter the room. Women are the mothers of generations. We have the ability to stop the continuance of humanity if we choose to. That is how intrinsically valuable we are. No, really, think about this...Women are born with value. I am not a massive fan of feminism. It waters womanhood down to competition with men and attempts to make women similar to men when God crafted us differently. If you don't retain anything else in this book, remember this: You are born with value. This world does not move or revolve around without you. The conversation of what you bring to the table is irrelevant because there would be no table without you.

Let me explain to you how much God thinks of you and how much he loves women. We are copartners in creation. Not subservient but copartners. Any man or woman who does not understand this misses out on a great deal of things. A woman is the ecosystem that nurtures life into existence. We don't just have a physical womb to birth physical children. But we have spiritual wombs to birth spiritual things. You birth the atmosphere in your home, you birth spiritual realities into this world through Christ, and things thrive from you. That's why it's so essential to flow from a fountain of purity because your ecosystem relies on it. If we allow life to flow into us and through us into our ecosystem, we would be amazed at the results. He also made us watchmen. You watch over your home and its surroundings, and you pray over it. You war for your family. God knew when he created us, we were the missing piece.

Let's discuss the number of powerful men who would not have reached their notoriety without a woman alongside them. I will never say "behind" them because that creates a narrative that a woman must stand behind her man in support of him and his dreams, making him an idol. A genuine relationship is rooted in partnership. I will discuss this ideology later on in the book, but as women, we are not only integral to our relationships; we make up the other half of it. Jackie Kennedy, for example, helped write John F. Kennedy's campaign speech when he was up for re-election to the U.S Senate in 1958. The speech was in French, by the way, because she had an affinity for languages. She was well-versed and well-educated. He famously introduced himself at an official function as, "I am the man who accompanied Jacqueline Kennedy to Paris." Michelle Obama was known to be very much involved in Barack Obama's campaigns. She was an exceptional speaker and did an amazing job of connecting her husband to his core audience. These interviews, speaking

Proverbs 18:22 He who finds a wife finds what is good and receives favor from the LORD.

engagements, and campaigning, all while still caring for their very young children, are just some examples of how she pushed his campaign and election forward. We could take it a step further and go all the way back in history. Marie and Pierre Curie pioneered in the science community with their research in radioactivity, giving us today X-rays, sterile medical tools, food, and nuclear reactors.

As women, we have to realize who we are and make sure that we are not chasing men that believe they are God's gift to earth. *Proverbs 18:22 "He who finds a wife finds what is good and receives favor from the LORD."* That "receives favor from the Lord" implies that there is a special favor that is given once a man finds a wife. (Now, I know some of you all are reading this and probably

76

feel as if marriage is not for you. That's fine; I haven't addressed that aspect yet. That comes later on in the book. Keep reading.) Anyway, you are a gift that must be treasured by your significant other. And let me tell you another secret that this society has lied about. God loves women. He adores women. As I embark on my journey with him, there are things he has spoken about me that no man or woman could ever imagine. God Almighty spoke those things, and they shall come to pass. We are essential to the world's ecosystem.

OK, I've laid out some facts, but let's have a real conversation. Men tend to exist in a vacuum of patriarchy, where, from the time they were born, they were told how valuable they are simply because they were male. Whereas women were conditioned to prove themselves. Display their worth and fight for the love of a prince charming. Now, what I just stated seems to contradict very much what I previously stated about women being born with intrinsic value and men having to build that value. But it doesn't. Allow me to break it down. Naturally, women hold value. Our beauty, our wombs, and our youth are commodities in this world. Yes, we as women already know that we are more than that, but that is not the point, and that is not reality. The reality of the situation is that those three things are commo- **Naturally women hold value**. dified in this world and if used correctly can greatly benefit women. All three of those things are correlated, meaning that, unfortunately, as you age, the world around you deems those three things less and less valuable. And to nail this coffin shut even tighter, those three things are naturally given to you as a woman. Men are a different story. In this world, men's status, wealth, and power are commodified. Those three things are used as mediums of exchange for other things in the world. They are a man's ticket to traveling through this vortex we call reality. But here is the catch: all three of those things must be built. They are not inherently natural to men. So here is the kicker...You ready? How have men managed to convince women otherwise? Or, as a matter of fact, convince the world otherwise? And force women into second-class citizenship? That is the kicker. They have not only controlled the narrative but also used women as allies by using women who also uphold this mentality. You have mothers telling their sons that they are special and any woman would be lucky to have them, even though they do not hold an ounce of wealth, status, or power, and can neither push nor influence the next generation to greatness. Imagine how many mothers have coddled their sons even when they know their sons should be doing better. Your son is not the epitome of greatness just because he is your son; yet, he has children out of wedlock, his finances are unstable, and his character reflects that of a seven-year-old boy. Nor is your son the golden goose who laid an egg just because he went to Harvard, graduated top of his class, plays lacrosse, and has a nice-paying job. And if that does not offer an interesting layer to the dynamic, add in women of all ages and races fighting over men who would make terrible husbands, are irresponsible, lovers of self, and have not one ounce of understanding of what true manhood entails. You have women out here literally prolonging the lineage of those said men. Birthing their offspring, who then cause terror on the next generation. If I had the world at my disposal, ready to praise me for every insignificant and bare minimum action that I made, I would also think I was the prize and feel the need to have women fighting and chasing me down. Why not? We are in a conundrum in the 21st century. As women, we have to regain our power and pick up our self-esteem off the floor. It's embarrassing. Once you have finished reading this book and completed the inner work, remember this. Make a man work for you. Because you are the prize.

Chapter Eight: Never Apologize for Who You Are

This chapter is a challenging one for me because I am still learning about it. This lesson in terms of hardship is up there with climbing Mount Everest. You know how some people never even finish the climb, or some have died trying...Welp. Welcome to this reality as you are reaching this understanding. I've battled with this very thing my entire life because I always thought I was too much of something. The encounters I have had with other women solidified my stance because I was unable to build the type of longstanding relationships I craved, which I interpreted as my fault.

There had to be something I could do about it. Maybe if I became extremely nice and sweet, then people would see my value, and girls would want to be my friend, and guys would like me. (Now don't get me wrong, I'm extremely nice just naturally. I am always thinking of how not to step on someone's toes. But I think part of that was social engineering by my parents, and the other part was just good old-fashioned nature. I used to be naturally overly considerate. Even to my own detriment.) Speaking up for myself became a no-no, because what would people think? I had to be nice and understanding so I could have friends or a man. I mean, who dislikes nice people? And for years and years, I kept getting burned over and over by different friend groups and by guys I would date.

My fear of rejection, and I suspect your fear of rejection, has created an environment where we do not have the necessary tools to guard ourselves or have the courage to fully be ourselves. You have not created a wall or barrier that can go up to protect yourself when you are in unsafe and uncharted territories. Nor have you made peace with the fact that no amount of open access will make someone give you love and respect. That is something that is demanded at the very beginning of a relationship, and if you are scared of being rejected, you will never fully embrace who you are, nor will you ever demand the very thing you crave, for the fear of being isolated and abandoned. You must be willing to walk away if it is not given to you. Maybe your childhood was one where you always had to take care of someone or be considerate of others. Or as women universally, we are taught that our aggression and anger are unwarranted, so we learn to passive-aggressively move through life. This can be seen through female friendships and dynamics that I started exploring because I could not for the life of me understand the experiences that I had gone through.

As stated above, learning not to apologize for who you are is not an innate feeling. We are not taught to protect ourselves. We are taught to conform and mold ourselves into our environment, whether that is a man we are dating, the workplace, or societal standards of what women should be, and even friend groups. We are not taught wisdom. I had to learn quickly to stand my ground when it came to men. But that was because men try it a little bit differently than women. They are blatant and disrespectful with it. I had a guy once ask me why I have all these standards for him, but did not have standards for my ex?! Sir, my ex is the reason why I have put boundaries in place...To protect myself! This is not Burger king, have it your way! Society very quickly taught me that men were villains because they were brazen. Masterminds, at that. And in order to get the life you deserve, you have to fight against their preposterous ways. They lie and manipulate, and a smart woman is keen to their audacity.

But women are a different monster. We are taught about sisterhood and camaraderie. It's us women against the world, so why did I need to have my guard up? They are my sisters, after all. Here's what I have recently learned. Phyllis Chesler wrote a wonderful anthropological and psychological book on female warfare called *Woman's Inhumanity to Woman*. Phyllis Chesler states:

> *The fact that someone is a woman does not mean that she likes, trusts, or works well with other women. Although women may be more emotionally expressive and interpersonally sophisticated than men are, some women also dislike and distrust other women.*

This discusses an interesting view of interpersonal relationships between

Our need to belong as women is greater than our willingness to accept who we are as individuals. women and a foundation to my current discussion of interpersonal relationships among other women and yourself. We are discussing the shadow side of female relationships and how those may have affected our views of ourselves and our acceptance of not only one another but ourselves. Women tend to be extremely cliquish, and we tend to shame and tame women in our friendship groups using indirect aggression, such as spreading rumors, isolation, or shunning, and at times resulting in violence; but that is minimal in comparison to the other ways we as women choose to fight. Requiring a certain level of loyalty and sameness among the group. And there is always a head girl in charge, and amongst that rank are her inner circle, and then every other girl, depending on her willingness to assimilate and her loyalty to the head girl in charge. The hierarchy spreads all the way out into the "least desirables," which are the girls who are allowed to mingle in the friend group but are not the ideal girls because they do not have that uniform setting that makes them blend into the group effortlessly. Our need to belong as women is greater than our willingness to accept who we are as individuals. As women, we are social creatures. Does this mean that there are no true sisterhoods and friendships? Absolutely not, but genuine friendships often begin with self-acceptance. And if you have a history of taming yourself to conform, you are most likely the type of woman whom I am addressing in toxic friendship groups.

Repeated trauma caused me to suppress myself just for acceptance. With men, I quickly realized that I was only interested in authentic interactions, not those dictated by what I could offer or how comfortable I could make a man feel. But with women, I didn't quickly come to that conclusion because of sisterhood and a false sense of security in my dysfunction. As I look back on my coming-of-age story, were there times when I was the perpetrator of violence? Of course. But were there times when the treatment I received simply because I was an individual was warranted? Also no. Here is why I can firmly state that your self-confidence and uniqueness will likely cause tension among women who lack self-awareness. I've experienced it. Over and over. I was not included in activities because I was unwilling to be a minion. Or women felt the need to humble me because they mistook my self-confidence for arrogance. Without them understanding that every time I showed up in my authenticity, it took courage because they and the whole gamut of mean girls felt the need to humble me over and over. Niceness and respectability politics could not buy me the golden key of acceptance because the running currency was conformity. And I did not have that. This is why you must accept yourself unapologetically. Phyllis Chesler states in her book:

> *British psychologist Anne Campbell notes that girls do not like girls who "positively asses herself or explicitly compares herself" with others. Girls find this offensive. Painfully--and almost constantly--girls scrutinize each other's behavior for displays that might be interpreted as showing that one girl is trying to differentiate herself from others in the group. To girls, as research confirms, "belonging" is the most important thing-- and in order to belong, each girl must ""conform to group expectations while not exceeding them."*

And we wonder why popular female social media influencers often appear to look the same and post similar content. People want individuality as long as it conforms to their standards of how they want to experience the world. We live in a matrix, a false reality that has been molded and constructed by the people around us. This is what makes conformity unrealistic and damaging to our psyche. There is only one of you. And although isolation and ostracization for choosing you above any clique may hurt in the very beginning, remember two things: If the people you choose to be around are not receptive to your true nature, then the friendship is not real. (And I know it feels real, and the breakups hurt just as bad. But girl...So did Neo's reality in the Matrix.) Secondly, remember that accepting oneself leads to authenticity and relationships that do not cause mental, emotional, or spiritual strain. Male or female.

Never apologizing for who you are is integral to living true to who you were created to be. But also remember to apologize for the things you do that have negatively affected someone else. I am all about balance. We are very much capable of being the perpetrator of trauma, intentional or unintentional, and it's vital to own it so that we can address ourselves and our actions. Let's all work on being the change that we want to see.

My goal for this book is to encourage and motivate women, including myself, to unleash our inner selves and free ourselves from the shackles of external expectations. And embrace what we truly want. Authenticity takes courage. Embrace rejection and brace yourself for it, but do not let your fear stop you from being authentic. We do not want to live a life of lies where we are pretending just to appease others, while crushing ourselves and our desires. That is a miserable existence.

We do not want to live a life of lies where we are pretending just to appease others, while crushing ourselves and our

Chapter Nine: Embracing Your Beauty Does Not Make You Shallow

There is this weird obsession with humbling women. The world has a strange fixation with putting women in boxes and creating and running with narratives based on those parameters that they assigned. Tall and dark-skinned women are masculine, short women are petite and feminine. Mothers should stay home and care for their children. We live in the 21st century, all women should work, and homemaking is for lazy women. Women should not lead with their sexuality; women should lead with their sexuality. The world wants a strong woman, but not too strong. The world also wants a soft and fragile woman, one who is submissive yet not too fragile. A woman should embrace her femininity, but not too much because…because…because… Everyone needs to BE QUIET!!! It has become overwhelming to exist in such a world as a woman. Not only do men push this ideology and these unrealistic expectations for their future partners, but we as women contribute to the abuse.

But you already know how we are moving in this book. We do what feels natural, and ladies, I am here to tell you that regardless of what the world has sold you and how the media has portrayed women who care about their beauty, it's all been a lie! Check out this double-edged sword. If you don't embrace your beauty, the world treats you as other, a second-class citizen. Because a woman is expected to present herself in a particular way. If you do embrace your beauty, the world creates a summation of your character and abuses you in another way. Do exactly what you want. Whatever vision of yourself you have, do that and be proud of that.

With that being said, I wanted to reiterate that your beauty or the audacity to embrace your beauty does not make you shallow. In actuality, the world is shallow. The world around you has, for a long time, pushed the narrative that women who embrace their beauty are shallow and evil, and cannot be trusted.
Think about the psychological effect that it has had on you. All the times you've looked in the mirror

93

and could've been encouraging yourself and calling yourself beautiful. But instead, you were running from yourself and finding outside validation. Am I being too loud, or should I keep going? Because the world has done a **With that being said, I wanted to reiterate that your beauty or the audacity to embrace your beauty does not make you shallow.** Beautiful job of gaslighting us as women, knowing that beauty is not only currency but a gateway in this world. But I have an interesting theory. If the world can successfully push two contradicting messages, one where a woman who embraces her beauty is shallow, but another where every music video, commercial, and movie has nothing but beautiful women, this can create confusing messages. Beauty DOES matter, but not for you. The common girl. Leave that to the pros. And herein lies the issue. Suppose you can convince billions of women not to embrace their beauty yet continually chase it because you have pushed a narrative that it is unattainable for them. In that case, you have a bunch of women who are willing to settle for absolutely anything and not barter their beauty as effectively in a world where the system profits off of it. Have the audacity to embrace your beauty when so many women are afraid. Not embracing your beauty and your desirability does not make you a rebel to the system or a martyr for women's rights. It makes you delusional.

Chapter Ten: You Are Valuable...Never Forget That

Let's talk about social value versus human value. Because often, as women, we measure our value by the things we have accomplished, the places we have been, how much money we make, and whether we are dripping in designer labels or not. Being a mom or a wife. Those are some of the most common ways we measure our value in this world. What exactly do we notice as we list all of these things? All of them have to do with outside factors that are separate from your being. They all go into the category of social value. Social value is the quantification of the relative importance that people place on the changes they experience in their lives. And these are all beautiful things, and they bring extreme happiness and a sense of fulfilment in one's life, but that does not successfully establish how **valuable** you are. Human value is totally different. Value is the regard that something is held to deserve; the importance, worth, or usefulness of something.

Your mere existence is regarded as valuable in the grand scheme of things. Your creator saw fit to form you and saw you as necessary, beneficial, and worthy outside of your social value. Social value is built. Human value is given.

This is how we must think in terms of ourselves. There's a lot of noise out there. Bombarding us with the vision of what value looks like, and we measure ourselves off of that metric. We must remember that ego fuels social status, consumerism validates social status, and culture reinforces social esteem. Human value has nowhere to go in those confines. Our human value holds more weight than our social value, because everything can be stripped from us as individuals and we would still be

We must remember that ego fuels social status, consumerism validates social status and culture reinforces social

valuable. Our value is out of the realm of what others deem worthy. For the Lord says, *"Since you are precious and honored in my sight, and because I love you, I will give people in exchange for you, nations in exchange for your life" Isaiah 43:4.* People in exchange for you and nations in exchange for your life! He is not being figurative. Now you may ask yourself why in the world would he do that? Do you understand that when he created you, he didn't create a bust? He created you with him in mind. He created all other living things after their own kind. Fish after fish, dogs after dogs, birds after birds. But humans were not created human after human. They were created and fashioned after the almighty. *Genesis 1:27 "So God created mankind in his own image, in the image of God he created them; male and female he created them.:* Imagine little ole you, fashioned after such a grand deity. Your ability to reason, your ability to create, your ability to rule and have dominion. Those are fashioned after God himself. That's why he would exchange nations for YOU. People for YOU.

Our ability to value ourselves also dictates how we value the people around us. *Mark 12:31, "The second is this: 'Love your neighbor as yourself.' There is no commandment greater than these."* How can you love your neighbor when you barely love yourself? Our ability to grasp the importance and pricelessness of human value also builds a stronger foundation for the basis of our freedom in this world. You cannot be truly free to exist, accomplish, and be if your value is tied up in the quantification of the changes you experience in your life. The truth is, when your value is tied to this metric, your self-esteem will not fuel your decisions, how you perceive yourself, or how God sees you. Instead, it will be driven by the outside world, which determines what is deemed cool and what is deemed appropriate. Do you know how many people chose a specific career for the social status it would bring, and what they thought it would do for them internally? As if working external to internal has ever worked for anybody. There are many people who married a specific person and moved to a particular neighborhood due to societal pressures. There is no arriving without internal peace. Even with that, you still won't ever arrive because life is ever flowing. And where you are today in a split second is gone because time moves forward and never halts for anyone.

Before we make external decisions, our primary question to ourselves should be: Am I doing this because I want to? Or am I doing this because I want to achieve this socially for the approval of a fallen world?

Chapter Eleven: The Key to Confidence Lies in Your Ability to Hold Yourself Accountable

Let's discuss how many of our insecurities and grandiose behavior stem from our refusal to face ourselves and acknowledge our most profound insecurities. The Bible says *Galatians 6:3 "For if a man think himself to be something, when he is nothing, he deceiveth himself."* Humans are allergic to accountability. I mean, let's really talk about it. We will find a mirage of answers that are outside of the scope of accountability. Think about how many people in our society refuse to get tested for STDs, and they know they have been ripping and riding the streets as if the streets are going out of style tomorrow morning. This behavior stems from not wanting to face the fact that every action has consequences, and ripping the streets is your action, and the consequence could be an STD. But the truth of the matter is that you need to go get tested. That is accountability.

We live in a world where we are bombarded by messages that tell us that every bad thing that has ever happened in life is the result of some outside force. It's someone else's fault. You are broke today because your mother did not love you enough, and your high school sweetheart cheated on you in the ninth grade. OK. Listen! Enough is enough. Where you are today, and where you will be tomorrow, and the summation of your life is rooted in the small daily decisions you chose to take that all together created a bigger picture. Are there a million outside elements that may affect the outcome of a situation. Yes! But we can't control those elements because

Where you are today, and where you will be tomorrow and the summation of your life is rooted in the small daily decisions you chose to take that all together created a bigger picture

we can't foresee the future. But what we can do is control how much we allow those foreign substances to taint our environment. Unfortunately, in this world, we do not live in a vacuum. Our lives collide with a million other lives a day. Our job is to make sure that those collisions end up telling a remarkable story of success despite it. For example, choosing to forgive the person who molested you at a young age and healing from that trauma is not for that person. It's a personal choice that you choose to make because of internal freedom. That said, the person does not have the right to dictate every action in your life going forward. How dare their malicious actions translate into the remainder of your life being ruined? No! You deserve justice and peace. But you also deserve healing. And you can't do that if you choose to marinate in their harmful actions. Their toxicity ends with them. Their attempt to destroy you for their own selfish gain ends there, in that moment that the action was committed. It does suck that you have to pick up the pieces and deal with the trauma and experience that hurt. I know all too well the feeling. But I'd be a fool if I let that person further ruin me. My revenge is my prosperity, my peace, my healing, and my ability to close that chapter.

The mentality of holding yourself accountable has to do with the ability to be able to say x, y, and z have taken place, but what can I do

104

now to evolve? I am dealing with this, that, and the other, but what can I do to explore the source of this thing so I can close this chapter? Before a wound can heal, the doctors must first discover that there is a wound. And unless we are willing to admit that the events in our lives have created an imbalance, we will never be accountable for how we deal with the aftermath. Never facing your insecurity of not being good enough may be the reason why you allow scum around you. If you can face this insecurity, it will make it easier to remove the scum around you. The enemy of growth is a lack of accountability. And stunted growth creates low self-esteem. Two plus two equals four.

This accountability breeds self-confidence because no one should be able to expose you to you, except for God. You should be self-aware and accountable enough to realize that, yeah, I have noticed this about myself and that about myself. This acknowledgement leaves room for confidence instead of an overarching need to cover your insecurities and unhealed trauma through grandiose and false confidence. If you can own the tragedies in your life and the insecurities they created, that truth alone gives you not only hope for a different outcome in your present life, but also an overwhelming feeling of confidence within yourself, knowing that the next step is to find the tools to overcome or cope. This confidence becomes a quiet confidence that is internal and separate from the external façade of flex that suggests "you have your whole life figured out." Because let's be honest. No one has their life figured out. But accountability helps ease the transition.

Chapter Twelve: Finding Your Footing Takes Time

I've watched many movies where women seem to have it all figured out. I mean, since high school, they already knew what kind of style worked for them. Their nighttime routine, workout routine, and what type of guy they were going to marry, and in what neighborhood they would be settling. If you were anything like me, then, idealistically, you wanted that, but you had bigger fish to fry. Unfortunately, you had a few dollars in your pockets, hopes and dreams, and a lot of acne. And here is the kicker, I thought acne ended after puberty. It is literally a lifelong thing! But I digress.

Fashion and how you choose to present yourself in the world are essential, socially. As women, we can't ever really escape it, even if we try. Finding your footing takes time because nothing is instantaneous. Rome was not built in a day, and if you truly want an authentic, pure self-expression, the evolution of who you are has to take place. And we all know there is no overnight quick fix. I never wanted to just scroll through the internet and find a random woman who had her life put together and then copy and paste her essence. Although plenty of people in this society do that, that is why everyone seems to be acting and dressing the same. That is honestly disingenuous. No one wakes up every day and wants to wear neutral colors all the time. There are some days you wake up and want to wear something vibrant because it's summer and the sun is shining. The aesthetic phenomena have taken social media and the world by storm because it's a cookie-cutter way of copying and pasting someone else's creative expression and adopting it as your own.

I will let you all in on a secret that I discovered a

Discovering yourself is the easiest way to find your footing.

while back. Discovering yourself is the easiest way to find your footing. If you don't know what kind of books you like to read, what kind of food you like to eat, or if you have oily or dry skin, then ma'am! How will you ever figure out what works for you? I remember when I was taking my natural hair journey extremely seriously. (I still am, but now I know what does and does not work for me.) I used to watch a million videos and buy a million hair products without first discovering what kind of hair I actually have. It wasn't until I discovered my hair porosity that everything started making sense. This one discovery changed my hair journey. I do not have a million hair products anymore, and I don't spend hours manipulating my hair anymore. I very much understand that some of this stuff may work, and others will never work.

Fashion, skincare, and even how you show up in the world are the same thing. If you are not a girly girl but love super feminine things, maybe a perfect blend would be mixing the two aesthetics in a way that creates something unique, specifically for you. Fashion and grace have to do with who you truly are. Who you are is a mixture of all the good and bad experiences you have ever lived through and the wisdom you've gained from that. That wisdom is what taints your view of the world. For example, you may never show up in the world as soft because your life experiences have

110

never given you the grace to. That said, would it be realistic to expect you to be as graceful as a swan? No, because I don't see a swan with the weight of the world on their shoulders. They look like they are living a good life to me, eating bread in the park and swimming without a care in the world.

But you may enter a chapter of your life where you meet the soft version of yourself through a life of healing, ease, and enjoyment. Is it realistic to say that you won't be floating through that river like a swan? No. Because your life looks different now, but your past experiences still influence you today. The best way to reconcile the two versions of yourself is by accepting both as you and moving in the world as that. Fashion and grace are closely tied to who you truly are and what you genuinely love, naturally gravitating towards. Discovering your true self is a lifelong journey. And here's the truth: I don't want any of us to rule out being a swan. Because as women, we should give ourselves the grace to evolve into that beautiful swan who does not carry the world on her shoulders. (Because we discussed that in chapter 4.) We should never shortchange ourselves. You can be a swan. No matter how unattainable it seems. You can be a swan. And no one can stop you but you.

Chapter Thirteen: Do Not Be Afraid to Demand More

Ladies...being a doormat will never save you! There, I said it. I can really end the chapter here. I feel like I said enough.

OK, let me stop being dramatic. The textbook definition for doormat is a mat placed in a doorway, on which people can wipe their shoes on entering a building, or a submissive person who allows others to dominate them. The second definition of submission is debatable because submission is a heart issue and not a being bossed a round issue. You can

In exchange for submission, you should always receive love, honor, and respect.

be submissive and never be dominated. If you are my darling, that sounds like slavery, not submission. Submission is always given and never taken because it requires an environment where both parties have a mutual understanding of what is actually going on. In exchange for submission, you should always receive love, honor, and respect. "Doormat: and "submissive" are not interchangeable words.

Scenario 1: You can have love for your boss and respect the vision she has for her company, and submit to that vision. Making sure that the work you do reflects that vision.

Scenario 2: But the minute she thinks you are about to type a 100-page dissertation and have it on her desk by tomorrow morning because **SHE** forgot her bi-annual budget meeting was tomorrow morning, you get it done. You don't let her know that not only was this stressful and unacceptable, but things like this should be given notice, or you will be packing up your box and taking your talents elsewhere.

The first scenario is submission—heart posture. The second scenario is that you are the mat that was placed in front of a doorway on which people can wipe their shoes before entering a building. I said what I said! Argue with your lace front!

We must understand this before discussing the need for more. How does a man fix his lips to ask for a submissive woman when he thinks submission equates to doormatting? OK, I just made that word up, but bear with me because I'm going somewhere. Being a doormat requires no prerequisites from the other party. There is no exchange—only one party benefits from the doormat. The doormat is an inanimate object with no feelings or say in the matter. Whereas submission requires consent as the first step and the payment of being cherished, loved, and doted on, on top of whatever other requirements the mutual party agrees on.

This leads me to demanding more from not just your place of employment or the men you date, but life in general. As we learned above, even a submissive person has demands. Only a doormat requires nothing. But a possible shower now and then, and even that is suspect because how many of us wash our doormats? The majority of us simply discard them and purchase a new one.

To receive the quality of life you seek, you have to demand the quality of life. Demand better friendships, demand better romantic partners, demand a workplace where you are considered human and not a number. Because truth be told, everyone wants to be loved and cherished, but no one wants to give up that love and cherishing willingly. It's too much work. And because most people do not even have the balls to advocate for themselves, how do you think they will advocate for you willingly? That is not a skill many people are taught. And people usually treat you how they treat themselves. However, here is the catch: to experience a better life, you must be willing to demand more. Advocate for yourself and your rights. Because if you don't, no one will. And trust me. People who understand the importance of advocating for themselves will not have a problem with you advocating for yourself. The girls who get it, get it. The girls who don't, don't.

Chapter Fourteen: If I Had a Dollar for Every Time Someone Told Me No, I Would Be a Billionaire

When you start demanding more, the world will tell you no. People hate demanding people. I mean. I have had so many people say, Oh, you're particular, or You are asking for a lot. Ma'am, I just told you what I do and do not want at my party. How is that being demanding? Did you think I would allow you to decorate the whole room with streamers?

You begin to notice that people love to put you and your ideas in a box. A lot of the things you ask for are not even impossible to do; it's just that the people around you have never seen it done, or they are too lazy. The truth is that they want you to exchange your ideas for their ideas and be happy with it because their ideas are easier for them. But not for you. They want you to put your happiness

119

in a box so they can give you what they want to provide you with. It's not only manipulation but conformism. As women, we have to learn to stand our ground. Refusing to accept mediocrity or something that falls short of your standards does not make you demanding or particular. It makes you, you. And the truth is, standing up for yourself and putting your foot down will come with lots of rejection. But you have to learn not to be afraid of rejection. Rejection is a part of human life, and the worst thing we can do is settle for something that we never wanted in the first place.

We also have to understand that people around you can and will be dream killers if you allow them to be. How many times have I spoken too soon about what I envisioned for myself, and no later than I stated it, I had someone rationalizing why the idea wouldn't work? Your boldness and audacity scare people. And your ability to execute makes them envious. My best advice is always to state what you want, and if you are told no, knock on every door until one says yes. Do not let up, because the minute you let up will be the minute you have decades of regret. Living life to the fullest means pursuing your dreams. There are very few times when your dreams are delusional. Like, are you able to be an astronaut without being a STEM major in college? No. The first step is to be a STEM major. No one, including yourself, wants to hear your dreams of being an astronaut if you have not first accomplished the first step. But when you have positioned yourself towards the execution and success of your delusional plan and that plan seems to be reachable the closer you plow towards it, go for it! Sometimes it does pay to be delusional.

Protect your dreams and hold them near, because people that mean you no good tend to be the ones that are always thirsting and longing for what you are doing next. And where you are going. So they can snuff the light out. There are so **There are so many people that were so full of hope and aspirations and heard no too many times and now are a shell of what they used to be. Maybe this is currently** many people who were so full of hope and aspirations and heard no too many times, and now are a shell of what they used to be. Maybe this is what you are now. Well, I am here to tell you, we all have experienced the naysayers. I kid you not. Before I ever accomplish something monumental, I always receive strong opposition. You are not alone. That is part of life. Along with our hope, let's make sure we have a close-knit tribe of people who not only hold us accountable but also encourage us in our endeavors. Balance is good. And sometimes the easiest way for us to lose hope is not having at least one person saying, "You can do it. Go for it!"

Another aspect of not settling is understanding that, in the end, will you be happy with your decision? After all, we all have to answer to God about the choices we've made in our lives, and answering to God for the things that other people forced or influenced me to do does not sit right in my spirit.

Chapter Fifteen: Being Smart Does Not Mean You Aren't Beautiful

This is for all my nerdy girls. Come closer, because I know you've all been sold a lie. Let me start with myself. I'm a nerdy girl. I love learning, reading, and challenging the status quo. I excelled in school, always graduated top of my classes, and can really run down a long resume of being the standard and typical nerdy girl...on paper. I come from a long line of women who understood balancing beauty, brains, and character. They consistently applied pressure. I had no choice but to be a triple threat—men's worst nightmare. **Evil villain laughs Mwuuaahh** OK, all jokes aside, this created unique circumstances for me because I never presented in the way that pop culture or Hollywood presented the nerdy girl. So, I could never earn the respect of my fellow nerdy girls because I didn't show up in the world like them. I couldn't sit with the popular girls either because, honestly, I was too philosophical and nice for them. Never cared to be a mean girl. Whether they were pretending to be shallow and mean to fit in or were actually shallow and mean, I'll never know. But I never really blended with them either. I was always an outsider because society didn't know where to categorize me. This world is extremely binary. You either fit in this box, or you fit in that box. You cannot be a mixture of things.

Your outer appearance neither validates nor affirms your mental state nor intelligence. Let me repeat that again, just in case you rushed through that sentence. Your outer appearance neither validates nor affirms your

mental state or intelligence. Meaning your fear of stepping into your femininity for fear of the world around you not taking you seriously is real. But imagine the regret you will have at fifty when your youth is fading and you're looking back at your life and imagining how

I want to state that your outer appearance neither validates nor affirms your mental state nor intelligence.

things could have been different if you had not been scared to wear that lipstick or do your hair a certain way. Only fools allow the outside appearance of a person to dictate the inner workings of their brains. Hence why corporate America is full of egotistical people who talk very loudly and authoritatively, dress the part, and wear glasses to reaffirm their position, but are complete idiots when they open up their mouths. We have a mirage of companies filled with people who talk a good game and dress like they are intelligent and have nothing up there. Interviewers gobble it up. Give them high-earning positions in hopes that their talk game is backed up by their ability to execute. And we wonder why productivity is at an all-time low. Be the intelligent woman that you are. But never think that choosing to beautify yourself and show up in the way that makes you most proud diminishes your aptitude.

People judge others based on superficial standards every day. And that is their own personal problem. Relieve yourself of their expectations and live. This is why one of my favorite movies is *Legally Blonde*. The world around her, including her parents, assumed that she was not intelligent enough to become a lawyer. When the truth was that nothing had ever motivated her sufficient to tap into her intellect.

Being dumb and not being encouraged to tap into your brain power are two different issues that are separate from how you look and appear in the world. People will tell you, "Well, if you want to be taken seriously, then...blah blah blah..." Oh shmuck. Did any of the women who chose to conform and appear conventional in the world of finance get taken seriously, or were the male bosses still hitting on them and accumulating sexual harassment cases?

The unadulterated truth is that people treat you exactly how they want to treat you. Outside of the physical manipulation that women engage in to evoke a particular sentiment among different groups of people, some women adhere to social standards of beauty to "fit in" and still do not attain or garner the respect they seek. It is a sad reality. This is why authenticity and true confidence hold so much weight. Tapping into that clears up a lot of confusion for you. Am I saying throw respectability politics out of the window? Maybe, but I am also saying always be respectful to yourself. As long as how you show up in this world is respectable to you, and you have your amazing, beautiful, nerdy brain to back you up. Who cares!

Chapter Sixteen: Figure Out What Kind of Life You Want and Reverse Engineer It

Reverse engineering, sometimes referred to as back engineering, is a process in which software, machines, aircraft, architectural structures, and other products are disassembled to extract design information from them. Often, reverse engineering involves deconstructing individual components of larger products. One of the hardest things in life is being able to see the future or anticipate misfortunes. In reality no one knows what their life will look like or where they are actually going. But having an idea of where you want to be is a game changer. Take for example the idea of doing math or research in school. Suppose you do not know why learning this equation is important or what particular answer you are seeking in your research. In that case, you tend to not only be off topic and all over the place in your research, but you also run the risk of lacking the understanding of how this equation helps solve the problem you have in front of you. Our life is sort of the same way. Our lives are a complicated mathematical equation and a set of research topics that require exploration. If we handle our lives in stride, where we take everything as it comes and we go with the flow without a goal in mind, we run the risk of never attempting to solve the equation we call our lives. Starting with the bigger picture (the kind of life you want) helps with the understanding of how each component (decisions) effects the final outcome of this bigger picture. As women we have to be extremely intentional about what we want. And if you do not have a vision in mind of what you may want your life to look like, you'll just be making

As women we have to be extremely intentional about what we want. And if you do not have a vision in mind of what you may want your life to look like you'll just be making decision after decision that may or may not help solve the equations of your life.

decision after decision that may or may not help solve the equations of your life. It's impossible to control every small component of your life. But that's never the goal. The goal is to understand yourself and the vision you want. And working toward that. Unfortunately, we often make decisions that do not align with our true goals. They are time wasters. And time is precious. I've had girlfriends who always wanted to be married. That was a goal of theirs since they were young. But their parents pushed education and success first above anything else. And instead of them recognizing their vision for their lives and then working toward that, they made decisions that, although good, did not contribute to their primary goal. They regret it. Hindsight would teach us that if you want marriage but also understand the importance of education and success, pursue both. Don't neglect your vision because your parents have a different vision or because society dictates otherwise. Pursue your education while keeping in mind that you also want a marriage. Don't sacrifice that for a career because your career will never fulfill you, because it was never your initial vision. Date in pursuit of marriage, all the while studying for whatever exam you have coming up. The two are not mutually exclusive. It is very possible to graduate from college with two degrees. A college degree and a Mrs. degree.

Another example is if you always saw yourself as a corporate baddie minus a family. Why would you make decisions such as getting married and having children when that is not what you wanted? Maybe it was what was imposed on you? But marriage, family, and career all take different levels of nurturing. Nurturing is connected to desire. And if your desire is not in the home you created, you are doing yourself and your loved ones a disservice. Now, if you already made the decision that I just warned against...Well, good luck, darling! Give the best you can to everything, because it was ultimately your decision. And you created the life you have today.

If you want to live a luxury-filled life, you wouldn't date Joe from the block, who is rubbing two pennies together, promising you something that doesn't exist, and you wouldn't choose to work at a low-paying job because it's easier. If you want peace in your life, you wouldn't keep chasing chaos and the people associated with it. You would purge your old friends and purge yourself from toxicity. If you want a six-pack, you wouldn't eat over the recommended calorie intake consistently each day and you would consume enough protein. We all know a six-pack takes consistency and discipline.

There are so many women out here who are not living the life they wanted but instead are living the life that was handed to them by their decisions.

There are formulas to certain things we want in life that require us to make better decisions. But we can't figure out what decisions we want to make if we do not even know where we want to go.

Reverse engineering takes discipline. It takes focus and it takes goals. Goals that rely on smart, calculated decisions. There are so many women out here who are not living the life they wanted, but instead are living the life that was handed to them by their decisions. Instead of happening in life, they let life happen to them. Have you ever heard people say, "Life happens!" and then they adopt an attitude like, "Oh well, it is what it is"? Don't be those people. There are more than enough stories of women who have made the right decisions, leading them to the current life they enjoy, or have dropped the ball but still managed to pick it back up and realign themselves with where they want to be. Your life is a culmination of choices. Women who you make lack accountability will disagree with this statement because it lays the responsibility on some invisible bogeyman. Without incorporating the insight that their choices in clothes, career, food, friends, neighborhood, men, and mentality are what led them to their "here."

And let me address something because this is not talked about enough. The victimization has got to stop. And I am not stating this to be mean. I can only give you what I give to myself. And when I am at a crossroads in my life, about to make poor decisions because of comfort, I give myself a reality check. Because I am responsible for where I want to be. Comfort keeps you stagnant. Poor decisions waste time. And ignorance is not bliss. A lot of times, our conscience will spell out red flags in front of us, but we choose to ignore them because we want something. Or we are attempting to manipulate a situation in our favor. This goes for that job you were supposed to phase out because you were supposed to study to get accredited for something else and get a better job.

Or your baby daddy, who, from the very beginning, didn't look like a viable suitor, but he talked a good game. Or your parents railroading you with their dreams and aspirations and forcing you to live the lives they always wanted, but you had other plans. At any point in your life, you can press the stop button and reroute. Do not birth and continue the lineage of a bozo who gives empty promises. Do not cave to the demands of your ancestors simply because of what they think or what they want. You have to answer yourself for the failure to advocate for yourself! Do not choose to stay in a comfortable environment at work, although you know there is a better opportunity that requires you to put in a little bit more effort. Where do you see yourself? If you see yourself at that job until you retire, if you see yourself as a baby mama to this man, and if you see yourself as the mule who accomplishes her family's dreams, then by all means, be my guest. You and I are here because of our choices. Make better choices because they protect you from outside threats. Your choices nonverbally advocate for you daily. Your choices measure the temperature of your mindset when it comes to the life you want to live. Choose wisely.

Chapter Seventeen: Marriage Does Not Have to Be the End Of Your Independence

Where should I begin? Perhaps I could begin by discussing how marriage can and should enhance your life. Or should I start with how people make poor choices, but then blame the inanimate institution of marriage? I think I'll start with the latter. To be honest, the recurring theme in this book is self-accountability. And marriage is not the same for everyone. We live in a society where marriage is becoming outdated and classified as a waste that's only for divorce and a broken heart. Now listen, I am very much aware that some marriages are toxic and should have never been a thing, but that has to do more with the people involved and less with the institution as a whole. Marriage should enhance your existence. You marry someone who is your best friend, who you do life with, and build and play on each other's strengths and weaknesses to create something solid—having someone in your corner who wants nothing but the best for your existence. Who thrives on your wins and works to minimize your losses. How is this bad? The cynicism about this institution stems from people who lack the ability to properly assess character. Neither do they have the discipline to wait for someone who suits them perfectly. Instead, they settle. And then create podcasts...

Marriage is not the end of your independence. If 1 thing that you want currently or in the future, choose a partner who genuinely likes you. Who wants the absolute best

The current you or the woman that you are fighting to be will need a partner who embraces and encourages your evolution.

for you and thrives on your joy. Because the person you were before them should still exist. What you have worked for, the epiphanies of your womanhood, should be embraced by that said partner. Not stifled and put in a box to stuff in a closet.

I like to think that the women who are reading this book are a lot like me. Women who are not only headstrong but also view themselves in their own image, not a carbon copy of someone else. And it takes a level of bravery for that. A level of independence. And that cannot just be turned off like a water fountain. Because once you find your voice, it's impossible to go back to that uncertain, quiet girl who was afraid to voice her thoughts and ambition. You...the current you or the woman that you are fighting to be...will need a partner who embraces and encourages your evolution. Marriage should be an added and welcome addition. A healed you can choose a beautiful marriage and foster your independence. There is no need to choose one. I felt the need to add this chapter because we have been taught as women that we need to absorb our significant other's entire identity to be submissive. We've been fed a lie about what being a wife looks like, which harbors resentment toward not only our partners but society.

There are supportive men out there. There are men who are not intimidated by a woman's success or her personality. Some men are all of the above and still very much masculine. They have their own jobs and careers and are successful in their own rights, but they are not afraid of you and your storm. I've heard several times women and men explaining how being supportive of a woman and her independence goes hand in hand with a man being a beta. But support and loyalty to the woman you chose have nothing to do with being a passive beta. But everything to do with what a good friend is. What a healthy relationship looks like. If you truly loved and respected your friend, you would love and honor their dreams and visions. You would help them accomplish their goals. You would foster an environment where they are safe to thrive. Anything outside of that is a horrible friendship, and a horrible friendship does not constitute a good partner. A good partner and a good friend are mutually inclusive.

Chapter Eighteen: Being Soft Spoken Does Not Mean You Are Not Assertive

This is something I've had to learn myself, as I am very soft-spoken. I can get loud, especially with girlfriends, but I'm extremely soft spoken when I am at rest. So, in corporate America, I got a lot of "I couldn't hear you," "wow, you speak so low," and "you should speak up for yourself." And people thinking they can speak for me or make assumptions about me or even bully me into submission. At first, I used to really resent being soft spoken. I always thought I would grow out of it. I never did. The only things that grew were my assertiveness, my need to advocate for myself, and my stubbornness. Because people constantly trampled the boundaries. Just because I am not speaking all loud and commanding the room like my peers does not mean A. I don't have anything to say and: B. I am easy to take advantage of. It simply means I'm soft spoken. I mean, I could be a whole supervillain with the way people make assumptions and treat me. It would not be hard to get away with world domination...

I'm writing this chapter because I am aware that I am not the only soft-spoken woman of my generation. This chapter is an encouragement to all my soft-spoken women that feel swallowed up in a room full of large egos. We must always be true to ourselves. And not

Do you know how much power you have to have as a woman to walk into a room and your presence and confidence speak for you before you speak?

in a superficial way, but more in an authentic way that stems from accepting your quirky uniqueness. This current culture pushes womanhood through the lens of men. Meaning we are encouraged to govern things and ourselves like men, push through a room, and speak up, or no one will hear you. Commanding respect stems from an internal presence. You demand it by your quiet confidence. Because confidence is never loud. It's always felt. Do you know how much power you have as a

143

woman to walk into a room and your presence and confidence speak for you before you speak? And once you open your mouth, it's a soft-spoken, commanding voice that knows her stuff. And now everyone in the room has to get quiet... to hear what you have to say. That's true power. Anyone can yell and strain their voice to request respect.

True power is respecting the rights and opinions of others while also standing up for your rights and opinions. That is the true definition of being assertive. Truth be told, the more you create boundaries for yourself, the easier it is to respect other people's boundaries. Have you ever noticed that the loudest people in the room are not only the most socially inept but they are also the least confident and trusting of their skills? Because the noise is meant to distract from the lack. Rest assured that being soft-spoken is not an Achilles heel. It's a superpower. Your voice doesn't need to boom throughout the room to command the room. Because verbal communication is only 7 percent, the other 93 percent is nonverbal.

Chapter Nineteen: Break the Mold

By now, I guess you have already noticed a powerful theme of this book: Break the mold. Where you are destined to go and who you are destined to be cannot be found in the grocery store aisle of Walmart or Target. It requires more than the average A, B, and C that the regular folks are asking you to do. Innovation requires you to go somewhere most people refuse to go because the system is always designed for cookie-cutter people with cookie-cutter success. And that is absolutely fine. But to do something you have never seen done before around you, you have to forge a path. Forging means to make, shape, or create. Everything that is the antithesis of a mold.

A mold is for people who like to play it safe. They are not experimenters or explorers. They never shake the room. They only recreate what was already created before them. Greatness requires a different formula that may create controversy within your inner circle due to fear. See, fear keeps many people from forging a path. This, in turn, later creates resentment and bitterness. Then that resentment and bitterness turn to jealousy when they see someone else who dares to go beyond what they saw. Don't be those people. You cannot be fearful of becoming an explorer and discoverer or a creator because all of life hinges on those three concepts lest we be beholden to stagnation. Evolution has less to do with science and more to do with life itself.

We evolve from small, helpless, ignorant children to shaky teens who then blossom to adulthood. Evolution means change, and you cannot change if you constantly fit yourself into a mold. Sometimes our minds are our own molds

You cannot be fearful of becoming an explorer and discoverer or a creator. Because all of life hinges on those three concepts lest we be beholden to

that resist the very change we need to become the woman we want to be. Those are known as spiritual strongholds *"The weapons we fight with* *are not the weapons of the world. On the contrary, **they have divine power to demolish strongholds**. We demolish arguments and every pretension that sets itself up against the knowledge of God, and **we take captive every thought to make it obedient to Christ**." 2 Corinthians 10:4-5.* Take those thoughts captive and make them obedient to Christ. What did Christ say about you? Who does he say you are? What about this and that, and what if this goes wrong? And really, your mind is telling you, "I am scared." But that fear ends up costing you years and decades of progress. For example, my story of how I became an engineer is unorthodox. Most people go to school, get an engineering degree, and then feel qualified to apply to an engineering role. I did the opposite. I forged my own path. This path was brutal and included lots of sleepless nights, but I was itching for a different narrative than the one I was sold through the education system. I got a degree in a totally different field of study, and fear pushed me to continue my post-grad degree in the school of engineering at three different colleges I applied to and got accepted to. First semester of post-grad, I got my tuition back and nearly choked because I was already in debt, and this was going to put the nail in the coffin of my financial funeral. I dropped out, terrified, because what was I going to do now? My undergrad degree is not compatible with the career field I wanted to enter, and I can't afford grad school. However, I then decided to teach myself to write code and was subsequently offered a job with one of the largest firms in the industry. An engineer designs and builds. Not only did I design and build as a job description, but also as a lifestyle because I had to be willing to engineer the life I saw for myself by betting on myself.

Regardless of fear, always bet on yourself. Absent of delusion though, because if you can't sing but want to be the next Beyonce and move to Hollywood...Ma'am, we have bigger fish to fry. The moral of the story is to filter your thoughts. Take them captive, or they will imprison you. Lastly, *"Finally, brothers and sisters, whatever is true, whatever is noble, whatever is right, whatever is pure, whatever is lovely, whatever is admirable—if anything is excellent or praiseworthy—think about such things." Philippians 4:8.*

Chapter Twenty: Never Beg Anyone to Be in Your Life

I believe this mantra is another tough concept to grasp as a human, and more so, a woman. Because we run in packs, it's extremely hard to grasp the idea of people genuinely not liking you for no fault of your own. I would like to nuance this statement for the victimhood mentality type people in saying, "There are times when you have done something to offend or you have wronged someone. Those times do not count for this particular situation." To elaborate further on my primary point, rejection can stem from multiple avenues, such as misunderstanding, refusal to understand, assumptions, differences, and fear. Phyllis Chesler's *Woman's Inhumanity to Woman* states:

> *The second explanation given was that of vulnerability. If a girl is a newcomer, has few friends or no new friends, does not have the right friends, is unassertive, or is*

in any way different or geeky, she is
vulnerable to victimization.

I believe the most important thing we must
remember is that people see you in one light or
another, depending on how they think and
perceive you. Which has nothing to do with the
truth of who you really are.

With those truths as our foundation, let's
explore how challenging it is to relinquish control
over how others perceive us and how we are
perceived. Because the truth is, this is something
that we all wrestle with. I am currently wrestling
with this. Our struggle stems from our inability to
accept the fact that we are not in control of how
people perceive us. Our lifelong wrestle with this
causes us to strive for approval. We beg for
acceptance in multiple ways. And nothing that we
do alters or changes their view of us. This very
revelation is sobering. It breeds resistance,
bitterness, and anguish because we naturally want
acceptance. You can't make that group of women
accept you. And you can't control how they
perceive you. You can't make that man accept you.
And you can't control the way he sees you. Your
family, your workplace, and random strangers you

encounter also fit in this category. It's a losing battle because the truth be told, people have already categorized you within the first few minutes of meeting you.

Our job is to have some worth. A person may not know what a diamond looks like, but that doesn't stop the diamond from being a diamond. Don't minimize yourself or ridicule yourself for someone else's foolishness. They didn't know they were in the presence of something rare. We have to bury the expectations we have of others. We are expecting things from people who can't fulfill them. We are expecting people to do things they aren't equipped to do. They simply do not have the range. It takes forgiveness to be able to release that person from the expectations that you have of them. So that you can not only release them but also free yourself. We are remaining in bondage and tormenting ourselves over and over by either constantly trying to explain ourselves through our actions or choices. Or the constant mental replaying of the situations that trigger us. Release them so you can release yourself.

There are people out there who are right for you. People who will understand you. Who will choose the truth rather than a carbon lie. People who will choose you. Life

Let people write their own stories. Stop trying to create narratives for people.

flows so much easier when you are paired with the right people. One of the most powerful things that I learned is that

people may be nice. But that doesn't mean they are kind. Nice means to be agreeable, pleasant. Whereas kindness means having or showing a friendly, generous, and considerate nature, or affectionate or loving behavior. Notice how drastically different the two are. Nice is associated with a performative act, whereas kindness is related to the nature or essence of a person. You can meet a reserved, standoffish person who is kind, just like you can meet a charismatic person who is not so kind. Understanding the difference keeps you open and pleasant, but stops you from giving too much of yourself too early. Because the truth is, a lot of people are wolves dressed in sheep's clothing. Let people write their own stories. Please stop trying to create narratives for people when they are showing and telling you who they are. Believe them. From the time we were children to womanhood, we have been taught to perform for social acceptance. But only a few of us have grasped the importance of kindness. Throughout your healing journey, guard your heart. So the people who really matter get the best of you. And so that you yourself are not participating in victimization: the act of singling (someone) out for cruel or unjust treatment.

Another deeper aspect is abandonment. And no, abandonment and rejection are not the same thing. Go figure! You may battle with one or both, and healing is a lot more complex than sitting in front of the mirror and saying you are worthy a hundred times. The truth is, abandonment makes it a lot harder to relinquish control over how people view us, because that control is tied to being seen. That control manufactures a buffer to prevent neglect. Here is what I've learned.

We are three-part beings in one, just like God, because we were created in his image. I digress. We are made up of a body: flesh, blood, bones. Soul: will, intellect, emotions. Spirit: intuition and heart. Rejection is a wound of the soul. In contrast, abandonment is a wound of the spirit. Wounds of the soul affect your emotions, intellect, and will. Learning to deal with your anger, or facing your fears, or addressing the pain of being rejected by a friend group. All soul wound. Forgiveness and repentance help heal those wounds, bringing about maturity. Whereas wounds of the spirit, well, those are a little difficult to address, and they affect your heart. They affect the core of a person's being and their ability to relate to God. Because I didn't understand the difference, I tried dealing with abandonment the same way I dealt with rejection, to no avail. Abandonment is a deep neglect of the essence and being of another human. This abandonment is exhibited through physical, spiritual, and/or mental abuse. But either way, abuse is always at the core. I was reading a blog post by Poema Chronicles that stated, *"Rejection is you aren't good enough. Abandonment is...you are trash and you are utterly alone."* As the article discussed, Jesus also felt abandonment, resulting in him relinquishing his spirit. For the first time ever, he was separated from the father. And that was too much to bear.

On this journey of recovery from abandonment, I have realized that reconnecting to my father and allowing him to resurrect my spirit has been my only hope. Psalms 34:18 says, "*The Lord is close to the brokenhearted and saves those who are crushed in spirit.*" No longer do you remain hopeless and isolated, but you become a part of his community. I took Poema Chronicles' advice and prayed for the healing and resurrection of my spirit. The spirit of God had to show me myself. If you are adamant about deeper restoration, ask him to reveal your truth also. Because in addressing abandonment, whether it was from your parents and loved ones or your community, you allow God to restore your spirit so that you can exist in this world as you were intended to be.

Not hopelessly giving up your will to live or compromising your value to be seen. Because God sees you. In closing this chapter, I will leave you with this scripture that has blessed me: "*Brothers and sisters, think of what you were when you were called. Not many of you were wise by human standards; not many were influential; not many were of noble birth. But God chose the foolish things of the world to shame the wise; God chose the weak things of the world to shame the strong. God chose the lowly things of this world and the despised things—and the things that are not—to nullify the things that are, so that no one may boast before him. It is because of him that you are in Christ Jesus, who has become for us wisdom from God—that is, our righteousness, holiness and redemption. Therefore, as it is written: "Let the one who boasts boast in the Lord." 1 Corinthians 1:27-31.*

Chapter Twenty-One: Femininity Is an Art Form...Master It

The essence of being. Femininity is so rare and misunderstood because we as women think femininity is an aesthetic. In an era where everything is an aesthetic and costumes are worn to portray that aesthetic, the state of being is rare. And then we wonder why everyone comes off so fake and inauthentic. Lesson number one: Femininity is something you are. Not something you can put on.

Lesson number two: Femininity is delicate. I often compare it to orchids or other delicate flowers because if the environment is not right, you risk ruining it. To achieve true femininity, you must dig deep within yourself and tend to your inner garden. Becoming feminine will require you to heal from wounds you may not have even known existed. You have to go through a season of pruning and purging and uprooting weeds that threaten not only the viable flowers currently in your garden, but the new seeds you are currently planting.

Femininity not only requires you to do the work and tend to your garden, but it requires the proper soil. Your

And now you see why femininity is so expensive.

friends, family, loved ones, and partner can either be toxic soil or fertilized, prosperous soil. It's like swimming against the currents in the ocean. You drown because you are exerting the energy to fight the currents to progress instead of swimming with the currents. Allowing the currents to push your progress. Your environment either feeds your progress or causes malnutrition. Femininity cannot thrive in that environment.

Lesson number three: Femininity oozes from the softest and most vulnerable part of who you are, and, unfortunately, trauma hardens your heart. Bruises your ego and throws you into a state of survival mode. And the truth is, some of us have managed to retain more of that delicate, optimistic innocence better than others. When I say innocence, I don't mean sexually. I mean a childlike optimism that you can be anything you want to be and go anywhere you want to go. That girliness that makes you run through a field and allows your feet to touch the grass as you walk through. The girliness that causes you to laugh hysterically at some joke you said internally or smile sheepishly when a guy says you are beautiful. That carefree part of us is still in us, underneath the layers of pain, disappointment, rejection, and lies. She is still there. But she only thrives in a safe environment. One where healing and revitalization took place.

Femininity is synonymous with vulnerability. And vulnerability is a man's kryptonite. How do you sway the movements of the room around you as a woman? Femininity. That's why it's an art form. It's a grace and elegance that comes from self-assurance and comfort in one's skin. Having the courage to embrace and love the very you. Femininity is simply you making peace with yourself. Obliterating the internal battle of constantly searching and seeking and never finding...And now you see why femininity is so expensive. It requires layers to be broken down so that you can get to her. The inner you that was always there but was silenced by the many voices in your head that rose from outside adversity. Making you feel that you were not enough.

Femininity becomes you when you start seeing yourself as delicate, worthy, soft, and deserving. Being resilient, self-sufficient, and capable are not mutually exclusive to this but do not allow the current narrative in our culture to derail you from precisely what I am saying. Femininity is not your enemy. Instead, it is your power. Learning to rest means unlearning the lies that women who have been scorned and disappointed, and lived in a scarcity mindset, have sold you since childhood. The evidence of such say women are how their lives are never ones that you or I would willfully emulate. We deserve a different narrative.

When you embrace the parts of you that cry when you are heartbroken, and that laugh and play when you feel silly, you release the stress of the world. The burdens that the world has laid on your shoulders, and you tend to live free. It de-ages you. What we don't understand as women is that the brutality we incur over our lifetimes wreaks havoc on our physical appearance, immune system, and

163

mental health. We must choose more kindness for ourselves. Your sensitivity cannot be overridden. It is what allows you to gauge danger and steer clear of red flags that a stone heart would ignore. Femininity is listening to your rhythm and dancing to it, not overriding it with the world's masculinity and abrasiveness. Because no one. And I mean no one. Suffers but you. Smell the roses, darling. What do they smell like?

Chapter Twenty-Two: Being Self-Righteous Will Hold You Back From Growth

How exactly does a metamorphosis take place in nature? An insect's or an amphibian's biological body is reaching maturity and therefore transformation not only begins to take place biologically but also physically. Each metamorphosis requires a realization. If biology did not signal a time for change, then a metamorphosis would never occur. Self-righteousness is characterized by a certainty, especially an unfounded one, that one is totally correct or morally superior. This certainty is the antithesis of change and evolution. One who is totally correct or morally superior does not need to change because they are the standard. But guess what? No one is the standard. No one is ever totally correct or morally superior. Self-righteousness stems from pride, and pride hinders growth. To grow, you must admit there are faults.

We live in a world that is fueled by pride and ego. Even as women, we find ourselves stuck in our ways because we think it's best. Have you ever been around a woman while you all were getting ready, and she was a little heavy-handed on the foundation and blush? Things are not blended correctly, and the shade of foundation is more than questionable...and you attempt to offer a helping hand to smooth things over, but she tells you she's good. Well, we have all been her before. Maybe not in makeup, but maybe clothes, or hair, relationship advice, or attitude. The point I'm trying to make is we need to remain humble in order to be the people that we always wanted to be. Constructive criticism is not a bad thing. Now, this is incredibly nuanced because some people do mean you harm and are being critical from a place of negativity, jealousy, and envy. But my hope is that as we age, we can fine-tune our discernment to notice who is who. But to remain on topic, we have to be open to constructive criticism, rejection, and teaching because iron sharpens iron. We remain rough drafts our whole lives, and with each new edit and proofread, we become better versions of ourselves. No one writes a perfect version the first time around. However, it requires being humble and a willingness to accept criticism from people with a fresh perspective. We must always strive for better versions of ourselves as women.

Being humble has a lot to do with realizing that although you know something.... You don't know anything at all. Here's a better description. Have you ever travelled? I mean, really traveled like traveling the world. When you travel outside of your ecosystem, you see how small you are. How minuscule your thinking is, and how much more of the world there is to explore. In that realization, you open up your thinking and become more understanding of different cultures and the people who comprise them. You realize that your favorite dish isn't even from your childhood, and you would've never discovered it had you not tried something different. But trying something different required you to be humble in your heart by saying, "I do not know if I do or do not like this, so let me try it."

Discoveries fuel innovation, and innovation fuels growth. Some of the most significant discoveries have come from curiosity, and curiosity is always free from pride and ego. This is the stance we must take if we are interested in personal, spiritual, emotional, or even relational growth. Growth requires an environment void of self-righteousness because the truth is, you don't know everything. And you pushing forth like you do will be the exact reason why you become stagnant in your life. Women of great caliber always approach a situation from a viewpoint of wanting to learn. Because learning is an indefinite thing, some of the wisest women you meet are ever curious, learning, discovering, and challenging themselves.

If you ever find yourself complacent and afraid to challenge yourself, then you are putting yourself in a mental prison. I know women I grew up with who have yet to evolve mentally. Yes, they have careers, what we consider successful; some are married, others are "highly educated" and have done the occasional travel to the obvious places around the world. And they have yet to evolve mentally. They still address people and approach situations like we were in middle or high school. The cause of this is that, although they have been moving through life and changing chapters, they have not been absorbing the lessons of life. They have not allowed experience to mold them, and they have remained rigid in their thinking. Listen, with age comes wisdom. And wisdom tells you yes,

1+1=2, but so does 1x2 and 2x1. You get the same results. Just different placements and at times a different equation is needed.

Do not be rigid in your thinking. Remain fluid. A stiff and rigid plank is more likely to snap than a rubber band. And don't get me wrong, being humble and ever evolving is underrated because this world runs on ego. People will play in your face. But I'll let you in on a little secret. Evolving is for you and benefits you.

The people who choose being self-righteous over exploration are not only fragile beings whose self-delusions are the glue that holds together their egos.

The people who choose being self-righteous over exploration are not only fragile beings whose self-delusions are the glue that holds together their egos. But they are fearful, brittle, unyielding, and have low self-esteem. You have to be an extremely fragile individual to be afraid to admit that you are wrong. To be so prideful that you peak because you are your own worst enemy. They know it, and you see it. Meaning the people around them see their mediocrity because of their pride. We see how they are not evolving. As you navigate adversity from people like this, you and others around you will also notice your own evolution. That may or may not create even more controversy among your peers. But who cares? Your growth helps fuel the life you envision for yourself and makes it a reality, rather than a dream. Besides, you can't be the best without being the best. Michael Jordan was never considered the best in high school. However, throughout his successful career, he mastered the art of learning, practicing, and being thirsty for growth. That is the only way you become who you see yourself being. People love to compare LeBron to Michael, but in my humble opinion, these two can never be compared. One evolved into his greatest, while the other was always considered the greatest due to raw talent. You know the issue with the latter? Where do you go from there? What records do you smash? How do you surprise yourself when you have already arrived? You don't. You become stagnant, which breeds mediocrity. The beauty of greatness lies in the journey itself. The falls you endured and the lessons you learned along the way. That is the beauty. That is what makes growth worthwhile. And that is what builds character and wisdom. Let's start accepting fruitful and positive change.

Chapter Twenty-Three: The Man You Choose to Marry Should Align With Your Brand

Listen here, ladies! We have GOTS to stop picking up strays, bringing them home, and trying to nurse them and love them back to health. There is nothing wrong with a stray, but sometimes, and really most times, strays come with more than we bargained for. Men are the strays, if you haven't caught the metaphor. And the majority of them come with problems you can neither fix nor handle. Put the cape down. You should not be attempting to save a man, but rather vetting the man that is in front of you. It is a man's responsibility to face himself and his trauma, instead of preying on women who are natural nurturers.

I'm never an advocate of preying on and hunting men. I'm old school. I believe if you want me...come get me. This keeps the dynamic fresh and on brand. If I am the prize, then I need not stress myself vying for your attention, because if you saw me and really believed who I was and who I said I was, then you would be working on winning me over. Why should I choose you over a million other men who are fighting for my attention? This is why this chapter is named "The Man You Choose to Marry Should Align With Your Brand." Because rule number one, as I said in a previous chapter, is that you are the prize. This requires a winner! A suitor may approach you; multiple suitors may approach you. The hard part is not having suitors approaching you because here's something else we aren't taught. Men will talk and pursue any woman. If she looks easy enough to conquer, then that's precisely what he will do. The hard part is knowing which men are not just pursuing you for the chase, but they actually see you as something valuable. The second rule is choosing. Choosing is connected to the word "marriage" here because it implies you have waved the white flag and have acknowledged a worthy suitor and his efforts. He has won the challenge and is deserving of you as the prize.

One of the requirements of the hunt is his being able to keep up. Are you on brand? What does this mean? This means, does he have the same core values as you? Core values are personal ethics or ideals that guide you when making decisions, building relationships, and solving problems. They serve as an internal compass of principles that guide a person's decisions. They are the breeding ground for culture. Have you ever wondered why some marriages last and others do not? If you look deeper than the scandals, such as cheating and money management, you see a more profound issue. Their core values did not align. The infidelity, the finances, and the disrespect were the result of roots that were never addressed. The symptoms of a bigger problem. For example, let's examine finances. Some people believe in frugality, and others believe in YOLO. Other people believe in working hard and pulling yourself up by the bootstraps, and others don't. For some people, money is a motivator, and for others, money is simply a means to an end. These could be core values that are not only opposites, but if one chooses to partner up with the other, could be a huge disaster waiting to happen. These polar opposites cannot exist in the same environment.

As women, we have to choose based off of our core values. Our core values will dictate the culture of our marriage. That must be our foundation, and once that is established, then and only then can we discuss how he dresses and if he's over six feet or not. Because, believe it or not, marriage is a long time to choose superficially. And let me add a little spice to this soup. If you have trash core values...And you know, because your conscience is always the first one to call you out....then throw it away. Get rid of them because those trash values cause you to attract like-minded individuals that breed toxicity. Then you are stuck trying to figure out how you ended up right back where you were before, when the reality is that you are the problem.

I've heard a lot of women say, "Men will do all of that just to come out here and embarrass you." The truth is, people only do what you allow. I'm not going public with a man who has not gained my undivided trust. The minute I see a red flag, he has to go. He's eliminated from the competition for my attention. And this is why vetting a man is so important. Truthfully, your years, peace of mind, and mental health depend on your vetting skills. We must learn, as women, to put men through rigorous testing of their character, temperament, and mental stability because any man you choose will not just be your partner but also the father of your children. The question should always be, is this man worthy of both titles? Or is he a clown waiting to show up at a circus?

A true relationship is rooted in partnership. The man you choose is and will always be a reflection of yourself, your mental health, and your self-esteem. I wrote an article a few years ago called "The Predication of a Woman's value." I discussed the correlation between a woman's value and the type of men she chooses to attach herself to. Now, this is likely to receive backlash from the majority of women. But this book is not for the majority of women. It's for the few who are willing to catch the gems and run. In this article, I state,

> *In all honesty a woman's worth has always been tied to a man and his identity. The idea that a woman must not independently breathe or think outside of a man is the driving force of everything. From beauty standards to minor insecurities of what God himself fashioned and said would be so. A woman's individual value is preserved as long as she is with a man who*

other men feel like are worthy of the competition, men of caliber. Take for example Lori Harvey. We think that her reputation precedes her because she is a woman that has chosen herself and has required standards that only particular men can meet. But this is not the case. Her reputation proceeds her because men have deemed her valuable because of the men that she chooses to entertain and attach herself to. Every new man is an upgrade from the old signaling to the manosphere that this is a desirable woman of value. This is a woman that high value men want so therefore she MUST be high value. If she ever chose to date Tyrone from the block and have his kid, her stock would dramatically decrease. Men love to discuss the fact that women can't find a high earning man if they are a baby mama. But the dilemma is not that they are a baby mama but WHOSE baby mama are they. And is that man worth challenging.

The question now becomes, what does your choice in men say about you? We can neither control nor manipulate the type of men who are attracted to us. But we can control our filter. Men show you their character. No matter how well they try to play the part, their masks always show cracks. It may manifest as inconsistencies in stories that are not supposed to be inconsistent. Or by the subtle flare-up of anger he displays when you don't do exactly what he says. Or the subtle remarks he makes on how he thinks you should or shouldn't dress. Your job is to choose a genuine individual. Pay attention to what the man says and couple that with his actions. Both give you insight into the soul of that man. Ask questions, notate his answers, and if needed, ask the same question later on in the future to see if he will

Fresh water will never mix with salt water.

give a totally different answer. A man's character should always be consistent. And do not forget the most important part of this chapter: Is he on brand? Because truthfully you can only gravitate to what you are. Fresh water will never mix with salt water.

The last set of advice is the most important: Allow God to vet the men you date. God knows all things, but most importantly, he searches the heart. If you lean on your own understanding, then deception is always imminent. Because the holy spirit that lives inside of you (if you have given your life to Christ) searches ALL things, including that man you have googly eyes over, he KNOWS the truth. I cannot tell you how many times the spirit of God has saved me from making life-altering decisions because of "love." His spirit will always nudge your spirit to let you know that something is off. And when he finally sends your other half, he will also nudge your spirit to tell you this person is YOUR person. Sometimes we are too independent and rely on our faulty senses to judge character and the heart when the Spirit of God is present and ready to help. He is there to counsel. And he is there to GUIDE. Please don't choose pride through independence. Allow him to lead you.

Chapter Twenty-Four: Learn to Mirror a Man

I thought he liked me. He said I should have his baby. I thought he said he's not the relationship or marrying type. But he's with her! Well, does he like me? Ladies, gather around with some popcorn so I can divulge a secret that will save you time, energy, and your youth. Men are simple. If he wants you...he'll let you know. That's it. That's all. As women, we often complicate situations and expect men to follow our commands, as we long for security. But here is an interesting realization. If a man is never scared to lose you, then you have already lost. If he has not provided security for you, you have already lost. And if he has yet to define you at all, then you lost.

The mental gymnastics are wasted energy. You have categories of men. Some men are attracted to you because of what you offer and bring to the table. They are the ones who loudly shout at the top of their lungs, "What do you bring to the table?" Because they need you to help them bring their vision to life. They have no intentions of assuming their roles in your life or recognizing your value. So, eliminate the notion that you need to prove your value. Some men have such deep-rooted trauma that one woman will never be enough for them. Those are called rolling stones. They rolled to your house and hung out until they gave you a baby, and now, they are rolling out again because they will never put their roots down. Men like this have also never established anything and never will. Some men are looking for a mother. Blame their mothers for telling them they are the prize and demonstrating excellent sportsmanship. They watched her suffer and toil, and think that is also your job. You aren't a good woman if you don't suffer for love. And then you have the narcissist. You can meet a man with narcissistic traits and tendencies, but he isn't narcissistic. A narcissistic man comes into your life to snuff you out and destroy you. So much so that you will not be able to recognize who you are because they are a black hole that has sucked you into their universe. And if you escape, because a lot of women do not, consider yourself one of the lucky ones...and you definitely need this book.

At the core of these men are gaslighters who selfishly interact with women for their own gain. I don't have enough space to break down every archetype, so I'll give you straightforward advice that will always save you. Believe a man and mirror a man. If he tells you he's not looking for a relationship. Believe him. He needs a woman who's going to ride for him (aka suffer). Believe him. He only does cheap dates, he doesn't believe in marriage, believes women were created to be stepping stools, tragically has burned every viable bridge, refuses to plant roots and build something, and does not have a job. Not only do you believe him, but run! You are not influencing this man to elevate his standards and beliefs. Nor will you be able to manipulate him with your beauty and charm. Men do exactly what they want to do.

Meet men at face value. Take them for exactly who they are. At times, a man may be in the process of a metamorphosis, but that process should never override what his core values are. We demand men with strong character. Not bums that are evolving from baby bums to bums with jobs, power, and influence. There is a difference.

Mirroring a man is the art of accepting a man at face value and imitating his behavior in return. We as women tend to demonstrate consciously and

Mirroring a man is the art of accepting a man at face value and imitating his behavior in return.

subconsciously how we want to be treated. Which creates an uneven playing field because the relationship becomes one-way. The only person who benefits is the man on the receiving end of your generosity in an attempt to show him what you would like. He heard you, and he sees you. He just doesn't care. And he's getting pleasure from watching you bend over backwards to show him this and that. Men do what they want. If he wanted to be with you, he would be. If he wanted to spoil you, he would. If he wanted to be immersed in your essence, then that's precisely what he would be doing. Men tend to show us exactly where their hearts lie. A man cannot be kept unless he wants to be. You cannot domesticate a stray. Cut your losses. Pick up your dignity and go. The best revenge is to gracefully exit the situation and not allow the man to harness your energy for his ego anymore.

Release the urge to want to show them and instead, mirror them. Imitate their lackluster behavior as you pack your bags and exit stage left. Do not allow a man to tell you twice that you are not a priority. If he does not want a relationship, do not force a relationship on him. Move on if a relationship is what you desire. If you want marriage and he's dragging his feet, then there is your answer. Save time. It doesn't matter the years you have lost. You are better off cutting dead weight and writing a new chapter. Time waits for no one. And whatever is on the other side of that door is better than the mediocrity sitting in front of you.

And last but not least, do not waste your time playing mind games. You will always lose. Men have an animalistic way of cutting their attachment to things to win. The more you play with fire, the more he's roping you into his sick, twisted web. Before you know it, you are no longer mirroring him to manipulate his emotions so he can choose you; instead, you are the one stuck in his web with clouded emotions choosing him over your right mind and well-being.

Chapter Twenty-Five: Sometimes Reserve Your Two Cents

This seems pretty obvious, but it's actually not. The majority of us women are over-sharers. We always have an opinion. I'm one of them! But over the years, I have learned that my two cents are neither always warranted nor accepted. And OOP! Guess what! Although you are coming from a place of love, it does not mean you have the right to offer your two cents.

Part of being gracious is knowing when to speak and when to remain silent. And trust me, this is so hard to do. Especially when you think you are helping. Here's the reality. The majority of people have already made up their minds and hearts about which decision they will take and what path they will choose. Us volunteering information not only breeds resentment from particular people, but it also cheapens your voice. Think about how many times a person was warned or given alternatives before they chose poison for themselves. It happens all the time. And when things go left, instead of that person remembering the warning, they turn around and attack you for caring and wanting more for them than they wanted for themselves.

People operate on the frequency they are most comfortable with; your words and advice may agitate their demons. We also need to acknowledge that people will only accept the truth at their current level of maturity. The majority of people do not want to live in transparency with their selves. Unfortunately, your advice may be too potent for them to absorb. As we learn to accept that, it becomes easier not to waste our breath. Let's normalize giving advice when people ask us for our advice, because someone wanting advice and seeking truth has a heart that is open to receiving. There's a level of humility that is required to accept constructive advice; Most people do not possess that.

I had to shed my cape, and you should too. As you evolve into your authentic version, clarity about yourself and the situations around you will become the norm. As this becomes the norm, your words will become more and more laced with understanding. Gauge who and where you choose to speak, because that understanding is lethal to simple-minded people and stupidity. Embrace your voice always but steer its sound in the direction you feel your voice will be more fruitful and necessary. Everyone will not need your voice. Not because the knowledge and understanding you have is not necessary but because your voice is only needed by a privileged few.

Embrace your voice always but. steer its sound in the direction you feel your voice will be more fruitful and necessary.

As we grow older, we must learn to guard our hearts and minds. Can we be sacrificial at times? Yes. But should we also learn to read the room for peace? Also, yes. There is always a time and place for everything, including your words. Learn to breathe, take in your surroundings, and relax. Listen more because listening will always tell you exactly what is going on and help you sift through the energy of the person. Listening may even help you understand the person better and what they actually need. Sometimes you'll discover they simply wanted a listening ear and other times they actually wanted your two cents.

Chapter Twenty-Six: Learning to Love May Be One of Your Hardest Lessons

Aaah...love...the art of sacrifice. True love stems from a fountain of selflessness. It's not a feeling of butterflies or happiness. It's a choice. A conscious decision. An action. And to be honest, the majority of people have, and will, drop the ball on this one. Being sacrificial and selfless is the antithesis of self-preservation and humanity as a whole. Survival of the fittest is a concept associated with Darwinism. This is how humanity has been able to survive. So then, how exactly, you may ask, do we self-preserve and love? You don't. And if you've made it this far in the book and have done the work...you may be ready for this lesson.

Learning to love properly requires you to step out of your narcissism and ego. Simply put, love does not thrive in that environment. If you have ever made a conscious choice to have fruitful and successful relationships, whether it's family, friends, or a significant other, then you know love has to exist for the relationship to thrive. Love requires giving of the most genuine part of you. Void of selfish gain and motive, and existing in pure trust that both parties are thriving in selflessness. Love requires trustworthy people and a safe environment. Here is something that we in this generation refuse to discuss: You cannot properly love from a place of fear. Neither can you build a strong foundation with someone if there are apprehensions because of your unhealed wounds. And you cannot and will not ever attract true love if you yourself are not giving true love. A closed hand can never receive.

We can neither right the wrongs of The past nor can we hold the future accountable for the tragedies of our past.

Should you always be cautious to protect your heart? Yes. But should you make innocent people suffer for your trauma? No. This book should have given you the tools to assess situations differently and recognize safe and unsafe people while pushing you to growth and healing. Because the type of love that we all require demands an environment that fosters hope. Hope is snuffed out by fear, and fear is the opposite of love. I know we were taught growing up that love is the opposite of hate, but the truth is the opposite of hate is apathy. And the opposite of fear is love. True love drives out all fear because true love is rooted in a certainty. And now you see why love is such a hard lesson to learn.

We can never experience love or fully give love if we are afraid. Fear is a character flaw when it comes to love because love requires transparency, truth, loyalty, and trust. All things that are antithetical to selfishness and self-preservation. This love I just intricately described is how you know if your family, friends, your significant other, and you love. Do not walk in fear of being hurt or rejected because anything worth having requires you to take a risk. Each person deserves a clean slate. Allow them to prove their love while you yourself are living by the motto of giving love. We cannot right the wrongs of our past, nor can we hold the future accountable for the tragedies of our past. Allowing people to write their stories is exactly how you can create new, fond memories and discover new love without tainting the purity of a new chapter with old, stale news. Love exists in freedom. Freedom to be while freely accepting another person and shattering the constraints of your jaded tinted glasses. This is tough. And can only be done once you have truly gone through in-depth healing.

Chapter Twenty-Seven: Learn the Dance of Prayer

I've mentioned prayer a few times but as I've been journeying with God, I've realized that although prayer is a buzzword in Christian culture, it's rarely understood to the point of intimacy. It's always used when we want something. Usually, when we participate in it, it's so brief that even if God had something to say to us, we break the connection before his words are spoken. So here is the definition of prayer. Prayer is the spiritual act of a human communicating with the creator of this universe in multiple ways. It's a conversation piece. Prayer is the way you build an altar to connect you to the supernatural. An altar is a bridge where the natural realm and the supernatural realm can intersect. It's a door. Not literal. But every time you show up to pray, you are setting fire on your altar and burning incense to heaven.

There are a few things prayer is not. Prayer is not begging heaven for what you want. It's not attempting to convince God of anything. It's not dull, nor is it useless. You cannot live your life to its full potential without prayer. You may be able to skate by, but the reality is you are spiritually dead without prayer. And it's a matter of time before your life force is completely drained. Prayer is like dancing the waltz. When the man leads and you follow. The man is the spirit of the living God and you

Prayer is primarily begging God to have mercy on you

are you, following his lead. When you start, you may not have many words. It may be awkward. It may feel like you are speaking to yourself, and no results are coming from it. But in actuality, you are starting on a journey to understanding how special God actually is. Prayer is a beautiful exchange where you give God your independence, and God gives you his essence, and in that exchange, your identity begins to change, and you begin to evolve as a creation. The way you see the world matures through his lenses. Prayer is an act of faith and trust. And perhaps that is why people don't usually participate in it. Because the reality is, do you trust him, and are you even interested in learning more about him so that you can learn to trust him?

This book and the vapid advice I've given throughout cannot save your life or improve it without prayer. And you cannot truly keep God first or get to know him without prayer. Prayer requires discipline because it's not contingent on anyone else showing up but you and God. Go into your closet, shut the door, *Mathew 6:6, "But when you pray, go into your room, close the door and pray to your Father, who is unseen. Then your father, who sees what is done in secret, will reward you."* Put your ego to the floor and speak to him. Let me break down a little bit about this *go into your room, close the door, who is unseen* means in this scripture. This verse is a gateway to understanding true prayer and intimacy.

Because the Lord is in secret, prayer must be done in secret. When we say secret, we don't mean hush-hush. We mean within the intimacy of your heart. The room is your heart. Within the intimacy and delicacy of your heart is a secret place where all your emotions, passion, and attention lie. That is where you pray from. It's not by big words or by loud shouting. But it's through connecting your heart with your words to reach the Father. Because prayers are not heard in heaven but rise up as incense, that means if you are detached from what you are saying or how you relate to the Father, your prayers will burn as unpleasant. Your prayers are intended to flow from a secret place. That place where your spirit, soul, and flesh meet as one. The meaning of true worship. That is how you enter the holies of holies. When you, the trinity—soul, spirit, and body—are in one accord in communication with him. That is when you sense him. In that harmony flows life.

Prayer is also dependency on him. You communicate your need for him and his investment in your life. Because without prayer, God doesn't have permission to guide you. Prayer is primarily begging God to have mercy on you. And in that, develops the fear of the Lord. Because your understanding becomes, if he does not save you, or have mercy on you, you will stay in the same space you currently are. And as we know, the fear of the Lord is the beginning of wisdom. *Proverbs 9:10, "The fear of the Lord is the beginning of wisdom, and knowledge of the Holy One is understanding."* Ask him to teach you how to pray. And on that journey, you will discover that prayer is simply a channel of life force. A place where intimacy is developed. And how love grows for you and him.

Chapter Twenty-Eight: Always Keep God First

I grew up hearing this over and over. Keep God first, keep God first...OK...What exactly does that mean? I was going to church and doing my five-minute prayers and maybe, maybe not reading my word. It depended on the day and how I felt. As a matter of fact, I debated whether I should place this chapter at the beginning of the book or at the end. Because either one would work. Foundationally, I could end the book with this chapter, or I could begin the book with this chapter—such a hard decision on what kind of tone I want to leave with my audience. I like to think that how you start is most important, but how you finish also matters. And now you see my dilemma. So I took a break. And after debating for a long time, I realized that the lasting impression was what I wanted to leave for my audience. So, this chapter was written last. Not because it's not the most important or was an afterthought, but mostly because I wanted this chapter to be my final words, because it is the most important thought.

Because I am a believer in Jesus Christ, I've been called through his free gift of salvation back into reconciliation with the father. *2 Corinthians 5:18 "All this is from God, who reconciled us to himself through Christ and gave us the ministry of reconciliation."* And in turn, I am tasked with reconciling people to him. We are spiritual beings living and breathing on this physical earth through our physical bodies. Everything we experience is spiritual. And this battle between good and evil is ancient. One that goes back way before the creation of earth. If you are reading this chapter, you are growing up in a climate where the name of Christ is being snuffed out. His deity is always in question, and in turn, people are exercising less and less love for one another, making not only the church cold, but this world colder. *Mathews 24: 12 "Because of the increase of wickedness, the love of most will grow cold."*

But know that nothing makes sense without him. Not the aliens touching down on earth, the racial divide, the hostility toward anything good in nature and productive, your mental state, nor the reason why you were created. As humans, we can't give ourselves meaning. We've tried. Which has led to ego and narcissism and an even lower self-esteem than we began with. You can't outrun the cloudiness you feel in your soul. It's impossible. And you can't mask the uneasy feeling you have with material things because you are a spiritual being living a natural existence. The earth sings his glory. And each of his creations has his fingerprint within their hearts, whether they care to admit it or not. We can never outrun God. Nor will God ever choose to force himself on you, because he is a gentleman and he knows that true love requires choice. *Romans 1:19-21 "Since what may be known about God is plain to them, because God has made it plain to them. For since the creation of the world God's invisible qualities—his eternal power and divine nature—have been clearly seen, being understood from what has been made, so that people are without excuse. For although they knew God, they neither glorified him as God nor gave thanks to him, but their thinking became futile and their foolish hearts were darkened."* Without him, chaos happens, which is why we have so much turmoil. Men have called themselves god. We've mismanaged our authority as caretakers of Christ's creation. Not only will we have to answer for our sins, but we are also essentially responsible for the current chaos in this world. The orphaned and homeless children.

World pollution. The hurt we inflict on each other and ourselves. And the only answer is Christ.

This book is a skeleton without the word of God or a relationship with our savior, Jesus. This book is a collection of bits and pieces from a natural experience. One that was only made possible through the grace of God. My experiences have been filled with hurt, heartbreak, brokenness, and pain. But Christ gave me a deeper understanding of my situation and then helped me through this healing process. You may walk away after reading this book feeling as if you have found the answers. But without Christ, you only have parts of the answer because your spirit is still lost and confused, and your soul requires a deeper healing. Remember, we are spiritual beings in a natural body. Our natural bodies allow us to go through so much turmoil from the world around us. But your soul and spirit take the hardest hits. Self-esteem is a soul issue, rejection is a soul issue, and salvation is a spirit issue. Every problem I discussed in this book affects your soul and determines your ability to connect with God through your spirit.

Keeping God first is less about creating a cute hashtag for yourself on social media. It has been the basis of my survival and the reason for my revival. Everything that has ever been spiritually stolen from me has been restored. *Hosea 6:2 "After two days he will revive us; on the third day he will restore us, that we may live in his presence."* We think wholesome navigation through this world is a physical manifestation we can portray, when in reality, it's an internal peace that no self-help book can give you. That internal peace then oozes through you from your spirit through the help of the holy spirit. And this may be a bit overwhelming to read and understand in a logical sense, but I pray that every person reading this gets a supernatural revelation of the heart of Christ. He wants us to prosper in every way. He doesn't just want us to survive but thrive within his good and perfect will. *Psalms 18:30 "As for God, his way is perfect: The LORD's word is flawless; he shields all who take refuge in him."*

Keeping God first is the deep understanding that Jesus Christ is the value. He is the prize that is to be obtained and sought after. And through that, everything else comes into alignment because God is loyal to those who are loyal to him. God loves those who love him, and God cherishes those who cherish him. *Mathew 6:33 "But seek ye first the kingdom of God, and his righteousness; and all these things shall be added unto you."* I used to read this as seek God because of something I want. For example, I am seeking God for wisdom, or wealth, or that new job, or a husband, or good friends. But that is not what this scripture is saying. This scripture is saying, seek him because he is God. No ulterior motives, and not because you need something from him. But because he is God. And in that you will learn his heart and learn to pray his will, which in turn will lead to an amazing life because his laws and precepts are good. *Psalms 19:7 "The law of the LORD is perfect, refreshing the soul. The statutes of the LORD are trustworthy, making wise the simple."* His word is the key to understanding the secrets of the universe. How to be a better friend and spouse. How to make and keep money, how to refrain from saying things that can put you at odds with the people around you, and the list goes on and on. But none of those understandings come until you simply seek him. Level one is searching for a deeper understanding of his essence, and level two is your life being transformed. Not the other way around. Any other way leads to a superficial, narcissistic understanding of who he is and leaves you empty. God does not exist because of you. You didn't make him up. You exist because of him. He made you up. Our lens needs to be refreshed in order for us to truly understand him.

John 7:37-38 "Now on the last day, the great day of the feast, Jesus stood and cried out, saying, 'If anyone is thirsty, let him come to Me and drink. He who believes in Me, as the Scripture said, "From his innermost being will flow rivers of living water."'" My prayer is that everyone reading this book begins to yearn for the truth and that the scales from your eyes fall. Jesus has offered us the opportunity to partake in his kingdom. Part of that is him leaving his spirit within you if you choose to accept. That spirit is the living water that is mentioned in John. Water has always and will always represent life. And remember, earlier I said this book is a skeleton without the word of God or a relationship with him. That is how our lives are without him. Dry bones clinging and clanking from one part of life to the next. The holy spirit's job is to revive you and flow through you like living water to then create fullness within you, where your dry bones are no longer clinging and clanking but now have cushion from ligaments and tendons and muscle and fat because he's rebuilding your reality. The holy spirit is the birthing agent of the triune God. His job is to bring forth new life *John 3:3-8 "Jesus replied, 'Very truly I tell you, no one can see the kingdom of God unless they are born again.' 'How can someone be born when they are old?' Nicodemus asked. 'Surely they cannot enter a second time into their mother's womb to be born!' Jesus answered, 'Very truly I tell you, no one can enter the kingdom of God unless they are born of water and the Spirit. Flesh gives birth to flesh, but the Spirit[b] gives birth to spirit. You should not be surprised at my saying, "You must be born again." The wind blows wherever it pleases. You hear its sound, but you cannot tell where it comes from or where it is going. So, it is with everyone born of the Spirit.'"* He is always ready and willing to birth something new. Allow him to bring forth new life in you.

Keeping God first is the deep understanding that Jesus Christ is the value. He is the prize that is to be obtained

Epilogue/Conclusion

Dear Beloved Readers,

I've thoroughly enjoyed writing this book and I hope it has made a strong impact on your personal outlook, your outlook on life, and your outlook on Christ. Every chapter is important and constitutes a life well lived. Remember that healing and deliverance is so much more important than everyone is making it out to be. And your ability to thrive depends on it. I am encouraging every woman to begin to do the work. Do the heavy lifting. Your body will thank you for it. Your spirit will thrive differently, and your lineage will experience freedoms you could only imagine.

As we reach the end of our transformative journey together, I want to share just how deeply your experience with this book touches my heart. Your reviews go beyond mere reflections; they are personal stories of positive change and growth inspired by the words we've explored together.

I poured my heart into crafting these pages, hoping to resonate with your unique journey. Your reviews serve as powerful beacons of inspiration not only for me but for others who will embark on this transformative path. Your words create a ripple effect of empowerment, extending the reach of our shared exploration.

In sharing your thoughts, you become an integral part of a community dedicated to growth and resilience. Your review is not just a reflection; it is a personal testament to the transformative power of self-discovery and personal development.

Thank you, from the depths of my heart, for being an essential part of this empowering journey. Your reviews are not only treasured; they are the fuel that propels this shared voyage forward.

With heartfelt gratitude,

Daniele Wilson

Bibliography

Chesler, P (2001). *Woman's Inhumanity to Woman*. New York, NY: Thunder's Mouth Press/Nation Books.

Acknowledgments

I would like to first off thank the true and living God for orchestrating my life in such a way that every tear, sadness, sorrow, and confusion has been to bring him glory. In his all-encompassing glory and might, he has put certain gifts within me before I was born so that my experience could somehow impact millions of women just like me. Because he is sovereign, everything in my life was meant to bring him glory. So here I am, bringing him glory.

My beloved husband, who has labored alongside me in love and respect. Who has created a most loving environment where I could find healing but also nourish my soul. Who sees the cracks and imperfections and still chooses us. Who has been my sounding board for years. My minister and my dearest, most beloved friend.

My therapist, who has been a very integral part of my internal decluttering and healing and continues to be. The one who sheds light on the truth versus what I may think. And challenges me to look at circumstances as a whole.

My parents, who've invested tremendously into me since before the day I was born. Who I am is a culmination of the good and bad experiences I've had with them. And their prayers have carried me here now. My life is a testimony of the promises God made to them.

About the Author

Daniele Wilson, an engineer with a Bachelor's degree in Anthropology, has turned her dream of writing into reality with this book. Her unique background enables her to analyze human behavior in a manner that is both comprehensive and accessible to her audience. Through her writing, she brings forth valuable learning points that might otherwise be overlooked in the vast tapestry of the human experience.

Beyond her professional pursuits, Daniele is a devoted wife and daughter. In her personal life, she shares her home with three cats and a dog. A passionate reader and knowledge enthusiast, she finds joy in the pursuit of wisdom. Alongside her professional and literary endeavors, Daniele also takes pleasure in cooking, maintaining a clean home, and aspires to acquire gardening skills in the future.